cover illustration by Martina Farrow

photograph David Woolford

photograph David Woolford

photograph Tony Rose

photograph David Woolford

Copyright © MCMLXXXVIII by
The Girl Guides Association.
All rights reserved throughout the world.
Published in Great Britain by
World International Publishing Limited,
An Egmont Company,
Egmont House, P.O.Box 111,
Great Ducie Street, Manchester M60 3BL.
Printed in Italy by G. Canale & C. S.p.A. Turin
ISBN 7235 6828 6

published with the full co-operation of the Girl Guides Association

£3.95

SO YOU WANT TO BE A designer?

When Justine Robinson's poster arrived in response to our 1987 competition, we all agreed it was a winner, with its clear graphics and message of friendship. The standard of entries to the competition was so high that in fact there were four runners-up, who all received parcels of artists' materials. Justine chose a boxed set of acrylic paints, with palette and brushes as her prize – her art teacher approved!

We wanted to print Justine's poster in the Annual, but the combination of shiny paper and felt pens wouldn't reproduce well. This was luckier for Justine than you might think!

We decided to invite her down to CHQ for the day and allow her to re-do her poster in our Design Studio, using all the specialist equipment, with just a little guidance from our designers.

Justine, her friend and Second, Aideen Nixon, and her mum all came down on the train from Liverpool and were entertained at CHQ. After a tour of the building, they tucked into a meal in our restaurant at midday – Justine has to eat at regular times as she is diabetic.

In the afternoon she finally settled into the desk specially set up for her and began work.

A photographer was at hand to record Justine's progress, and this is what he saw . . .

by Susannah Marriott
photographs Chris Phillips

Justine starts work; Aideen looks on. ▶ Our Studio Manager enlarged the original poster to A3 size, so Justine had something to follow. Using the board's parallel motion and a set square, Justine was able to keep everything straight. She traced off Letraset lettering to give her poster that professional touch.

Hints on design: *Keep it simple and big. One colourful design with lots of white space like Justine's will attract lots more attention than a bitty, detailed drawing.*

◀ On the roof at CHQ. Spot the Telecom Tower and Buckingham Palace in the background.

Looking for inspiration. We admire the ▶ design of some 1930s Guide Annuals from the Library at CHQ.

Justine learns how Today's Guide is produced, and is interviewed. Here we see how galley proofs are pasted up, match colour proofs with Pantone charts and decide which readers' letters to print.
▼

The finishing touches of colour. Justine left the colour till last – it's her favourite bit! She was given a huge box of Pantone colour sticks to choose from.
▼

Hints on colour: Keep it bright, using two or three basic primary colours. Again, simplicity is best – if in doubt, leave it out!

After watching Justine at work, we have great hopes for the future – the art world had better watch out in a few years' time!

Mocktails COCKTAILS

by Julia Nellthorp
illustrations Caroline Bland

Why not throw a cocktail party? You would be joining one long party – cocktails were first invented hundreds of years ago. There are almost as many legends about the invention of the cocktail as there are recipes, and nobody seems to know which is the true version. The most likely story is one which dates back to 1779 at a drinking hostelry in Virginia, USA, where soldiers used to meet and joke about the chicken farm next door. The owner of the tavern decided to stop the teasing by mixing a potent drink and serving each portion with a feather from the tail of a cockerel. As they raised their glasses in a toast, one of the soldiers called out 'Vive le cocktail' and from that day on the mystery potent mix was called a cocktail!

It was in the 1920s that the cocktail became really popular along with the Charleston, feather boas and jazz. Why not throw a '20s cocktail party and ask your guests to come appropriately dressed and ready to Charleston?

Cocktails tend to be rather potent mixes of alcoholic drinks but they don't have to be knockouts in this way! You can make exotic looking and delicious tasting 'mocktails' without any alcohol in them at all.

Try some of these recipes and make sure you have lots of cherries, lemon slices and other decorations to add the final touches in true cocktail barman style! You don't need a cocktail shaker – a clean, empty jar will do – but make sure the lid fits securely or you will end up shaking your concoctions over the walls! Paper umbrellas and 'swizzle sticks' are fun but not crucial. Remember to use the same measure, e.g. a small glass or teacup throughout and multiply all the ingredients carefully for larger quantities.

Prairie Oyster

Shake together 1 teaspoonful Worcestershire sauce, 1 teaspoonful tomato ketchup, 2 dashes of vinegar and some pepper. Pour into a glass and just before serving drop an egg yolk in the drink. Swallow in one gulp!

Tapestry Sunrise

You'll need to use an electric blender for this recipe. Blend some crushed ice, 1 fresh peach (or some canned slices), 1 dash of lime cordial and 3 measures of pineapple juice. Serve garnished with whatever fruit is available.

Honey Pie

For four drinks use 2 apples (peeled, cored, sliced), 3 tablespoons clear honey, 500ml apple juice, 500ml grape juice, a handful of chopped hazelnuts, 4 tablespoons of whipped cream. Heat the juices with the honey until dissolved. Blend (in a liquidiser) with the apples and hazelnuts. Serve a spoonful of whipped cream in each drink.

San Francisco

Shake together equal parts of orange juice, lemon juice, grapefruit juice and pineapple juice, and an egg white. Pour into tall glasses and top up with soda water.

Ugly

This 'mocktail' gets its name from the ugli fruit which is a cross between a grapefruit and a tangerine. Simply mix equal quantities of grapefruit and orange juice and serve poured over plenty of ice and decorated with slices of orange and slivers of grapefruit rind.

Cappuccine

Shake one splash of peppermint cordial with four measures of cream. Pour over crushed ice and grate some chocolate on the top before serving.

Academy Fizz

Blend 6 strawberries, mix gently with 1 measure of cream soda and pour into tall glasses. Top with a scoop of strawberry ripple ice-cream and garnish with fresh strawberries.

Mickey Mouse

Put ice cubes in a tall glass and pour in cola. Add a scoop of vanilla ice-cream and top with whipped cream and cherries. Serve immediately with straws and a spoon.

P😵P THE QUESTION

by Brenda Apsley

1 Pepsi and Shirley were backing singers in which band before going solo?

   a The Style Council
   b Wham!
   c The Communards

2 Fill in the missing colour to complete the names of three groups:
Simply _ _ _
_ _ _ Box
_ _ _ _ _ Britain

Are you a pop expert? Try to answer all twenty questions, then check your answers on page 63.

3 This Scottish singer had a big hit with *My Favourite Waste of Time*. Can you name him? ▶

4 Ben from Curiosity Killed the Cat has a very odd surname, what is it?

   a Vol-au-vent Pissaro
   b Monpellier Perrier
   c Volpeliere Pierrot

5 Who wrote the Band Aid single *Do They Know It's Christmas?* with Bob Geldof?

6 *Every Loser Wins* was a hit single for which *EastEnders* star?

◀**7** Can you name the three members of A-ha?

8 Paul Weller (now with the Style Council) used to be with which band?

   a The Clash
   b The Jam
   c Dexy's Midnight Runners

13 What was this American singer and actress's maiden name?

14 Morrissey used to sing with which band?

15 Which supergroup has recorded hits for a James Bond film and include a famous sailor amongst their crew?

16 Which all girl band had a hit with *Walk Like an Egyptian*?

    a The Brooches
    b The Earrings
    c The Bangles

17 What is this man's real name?

    a Michael Barrett
    b Michael Brandon
    c Beverley Barthes

9 Delroy, Lorraine, Deniece, Doris and Stedman are the five members of which family group?

10 What was Nick Kamen before he had a hit record?

    a a model
    b an artist
    c a waiter
    ▼

11 Neil Tennant and Chris Lowe are the two members of which band?

12 What is the biggest-selling album of all time? By Michael Jackson, it has sold more than 40 million copies.

18 Which girl singer had a hit album called *Control*? She has a very famous older brother.

19 When Jimmy Somerville left Bronski Beat, which new band did he form? They had a big hit with *So Cold The Night*.

20 Which country do A-ha come from?

Answers page 63.

Colour transparencies courtesy of Epic, Sire and WEA Records.

9

Two days with Treasure Hunt

A helicopter hovers above the grounds of a hotel in Wrexham; its whirling rotor blades give off a welcoming cool draught on this hot July morning.

But it's no ordinary helicopter. The distinctive white, yellow and gold is familiar, even from a distance. And what makes it really recognisable is the black lettering on the fuselage which reads TREASURE HUNT.

Clwyd Guides, Sharon Williams and Helen Jones, and myself had been invited to look behind the scenes of this fast-moving television programme and to watch location filming at one of the clue sites in the sixth series made by Chatsworth Television for Channel Four.

Our first sight of the team came when the helicopter returned to base after rehearsing the 'live' show. As the rotor blades came to a halt, pilot Keith Thompson, cameraman Graham Berry and video engineer Frank Mayburgh, stepped down. But who was the man wearing Anneka's runner pack and headphones? 'Oh that's producer Malcolm Heyworth', explained researcher Angela Breheny. 'He acts as Annie's stand-in, checking that the course is practical and safe before the actual recording next day.'

Here's a record of that day, when we watched the filming and met the real Anneka Rice.

One for the album; we meet Anneka Rice by the Skyrunner helicopter. ▼

The Skyrunner helicopter piloted by Captain Keith Thompson must be the most famous helicopter in the country. The communications helicopter is packed with technical equipment including four radios, costing some £45,000. Both helicopters carry fuel on board for only 15 minutes longer than the actual running time of the programme! ▼

by Michael Edwards
photographs Michael Edwards

We'd been given the name of one of the usually secret clue sites. Here we await Anneka's arrival at the 16th century Boat Inn at Erbistock, near Wrexham.

Are you on your way?' I ask Captain ▶ Michael Malric-Smith who pilots the communications helicopter. The communications pack which Anneka runs about with was as heavy as a satchel-full of books. I wouldn't like to carry it around for too long!

◀ We watch as Anneka plays the ancient art of Dwile-flonking. Anneka joined a dancing circle of Dwile-flonkers only to be hit in the face with a beer soaked rag – the Dwile! That moment was the clue. The clock stopped with just 10 seconds to go. Here Anneka gets her own back.

The day really raced by. It didn't seem long before we were waving Anneka good-bye.
▼

Here we are relaxing with Anneka during our interview back at the hotel.

The highlight of the day was our exclusive interview with Anneka in her hotel. Here's what we learned about her:

Helen How did you get the *Treasure Hunt* job?

Anneka They were originally looking for a man who was very fit; an ex-Olympic skier or someone like that. In the French version of the programme they have a very athletic male skyrunner. Somehow I got sent along to the audition by mistake. I think my agent was a bit confused. Lots of people turned up in designer track suits and trainers. I ended up meeting the producer and crew and we made a mini *Treasure Hunt* in Hyde Park. Graham, our cameraman here, was on that audition and he almost had a nervous breakdown as all these terribly fit people disappeared into the distance well beyond his zoom lens. When I trekked up at a more leisurely pace I heard him say to the producer, 'It's got to be Anneka – she's the only one I can keep up with.' Malcolm Hayward, the producer, thought it would be a change having a lady doing it and here I am.

Helen How do you keep fit for the programme?

Anneka I used to train with a three-mile jog every day and I have a gym at home. I'm really very fanatical about fitness. I find that in the normal course of my work I keep myself in good trim. On the programme you have been with today I suppose I have run a couple of miles. I keep fit without really trying. On *Wish You Were Here*, which I film for Thames Television, they are always getting me to do activity holidays. Last year I did a pony trekking week in Wales and I have just been cycling in the Lake District for them. I just love being active.

Sharon What country have you most enjoyed visiting with *Treasure Hunt*?

Anneka Bali. We went there for the first series. I'm very fond of the Far East. My favourite country is Australia. I've been there several times. In November we are making a *Treasure Hunt* there and I'm looking forward to that.

Sharon What is your most nerve-wracking experience with *Treasure Hunt*?

Anneka That was in Florida. There was a clue in a big top – right at the top. I climbed a ladder to where two trapeze artistes were waiting. I thought that I would just take the clue from them. But they grabbed me, secured me into a harness and pushed me off into space. I have never been so scared in all my life. I was terrified. I didn't know what to do, so I just swung to and fro for ten minutes and we lost the show. I was too frightened to jump even though there was a safety net.

Sharon What is your most embarrassing moment in *Treasure Hunt*?

Anneka People always remind me about the time my trousers split. We saw a man putting grass-cuttings into a wheelbarrow. He had a van, so we asked him for a lift to Wookey Hole in Somerset. He said that he would . . . providing I helped him gather his grass. I bent down to grab an armful of cuttings and there was a loud rip. I spent the rest of the run hiding my embarrassment with my map. After that incident several elderly viewers sent me sewing kits in case it should happen again.

Helen Can the weather be a problem?

Anneka We have been very lucky with the weather. We always shoot during a five-week period in June and July. This series, though, has been the worst. We went to southern Ireland and didn't get a thing done because of low cloud and rain. We'll go back again when we have made all the other programmes in this series.

Helen Do you really not know the whereabouts of the clues?

Anneka I really have no idea. I don't particularly want to. The first two years I used to put cups against doors so I could hear what was going on; even then I didn't know. It would be less fun if I knew where I was going.

Sharon Do you have any hobbies in your spare time?

Anneka Well, I really don't have too much spare time. I seem to work most of the year. When I do have a Sunday off it's so lovely to get home and crash out and do nothing except watch the omnibus edition of *EastEnders*. On location we generally stay where there are good sports facilities: a tennis court or swimming pool. I find it difficult to relax totally. I always want to be doing something or other.

Sharon Do you have a favourite pop group?

Anneka My 17-year-old sister has hysterics about me and pop music – I haven't a clue. They seem to have such strange names like Dr and the Medics and the Pet Shop Boys. I get them all muddled up. At the moment I don't like contemporary music at all!

Helen Do you get on well with the crew?

Anneka Yes, very much so. Working on *Treasure Hunt* is like going on holiday with your best friends!

If you would like to know more about *Treasure Hunt*, *The Treasure Hunt Book* is now available from bookshops or direct from Hamlyn Publishers, Twickenham, Middlesex.

We'd like to thank Anneka Rice and everyone at Chatsworth Television for their assistance.

PITCH CAMP ON A C·A·K·E

by Julia Nellthorp
illustrations Nicola Heindl

Slice the cake horizontally through and fill with ⅔ of the butter-cream. Use the rest to coat the outside. Colour 150g of the fondant with a tiny drop of green food colouring. Spread thinly on the top of the cake for grass.

Press the chocolate finger biscuits gently around the outside.

Crumble some of the flake bar and build a 'fire' on the cake. Colour about 25g of the marzipan with just a drop of brown food colouring and make a few small balls for stones or bricks.

Colour about 100g of marzipan with a tiny drop of green for the tents. Not too much or they'll be rather livid! Shape them and arrange on the cake as you would pitch camp. If you are feeling steady-handed, pipe some fondant guy ropes for authenticity!

A camp without plenty of food is unheard of, so create a pan-full. Fried eggs are easy to make with yellow marzipan yolks and fondant icing whites. Sausages, beans and bread are equally simple. Let your imagination run riot – the joy of this sort of camp food is that you can just squash it up and start again if it doesn't turn out quite right! Don't forget the plates, mugs and cutlery.

You will need:

1 chocolate or plain sponge cake
jam or butter-cream filling
1 packet of chocolate finger biscuits
250g marzipan
1 portion of fondant icing
green, brown and blue food colouring
1 chocolate flake bar

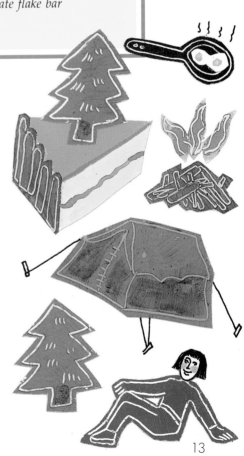

Shape some trees from green coloured marzipan – conifers are the easiest, but try out some others too. For conifers just roll cones from green marzipan and rest them on brown marzipan trunks, but try being more adventurous. Cut shapes and build up the layers of the trees. A more realistic trunk can be made from pieces of flake.

Arrange the trees on the cake and add a thinly-rolled pale blue marzipan lake or river.

This is just a starting point. Why not make buckets, flag poles, wellies on sticks, washing on lines . . . the list is endless! And of course if you are a clever sculptress you could even mould your Unit or Patrol!

SHE DOESN'T SUSPECT A THING

by Lynda Neilands
illustrations Frances Lloyd

Almost everyone in my class goes around in some sort of a "crowd". There's a sporty crowd, who play hockey, and a trendy crowd, who go to discos, and then there's the music crowd – six of them, four girls and two blokes – who belong to the Youth Orchestra and hang around in the music room at break. This time last week I wasn't part of any crowd. My name, by the way, is Sarah. I'm thirteen years old and would be OK looking if my legs were longer. Unfortunately whenever I buy jeans I have to chop about two metres off the bottoms so you can understand why I'm not rushing out madly onto the hockey pitch or the disco floor. As far as music goes, Mum did send me for piano lessons when I was six, but that was before I'd worked out which was my right and which was my left hand, so I never made much progress. I don't play anything now – not even the recorder – which is why I almost dropped dead with astonishment when Kate Forbes rushed up to me in the locker area last Monday and invited me to her house for the weekend.

Kate Forbes is a musical genius. She plays the piano, the guitar and the violin. She is also tall and dramatic-looking, and beside her I felt like an incompetent midget.

"Yes . . . well . . . er . . ." I wracked my brains for an excuse. "I'll need to ask Mum. She'll probably want me to visit my aunt in hospital, you know . . ."

Anyone else would have picked up the negative vibes and backed off – but not Kate. "No problem," says she breezily. "I'll get Madeleine to ring her and sort everything out." (Madeleine is what she calls her mum!)

"Great!" I said, immediately deciding to beetle home as fast as I could after school to forestall that phone call. But as luck would have it, I missed the bus and by the time I panted into our living room Madeleine had done her worst. Mum's eyes were alight with enthusiasm.

"Naturally I said you could go," she beamed. "It's high time you stopped mooning around under my feet all weekend and made a few friends."

"But, Mum," I bleated. "What about Auntie Pat?"

"Well what about her? She got out of hospital the day before yesterday. She'll be recuperating in Scunthorpe by now."

There was nothing more to be said. The following Friday I waved Mum goodbye and trundled into school with my most respectable A-ha nightshirt stuffed into her pale lavender overnight case. Misery must have been written all over my face, because Kate took one look at me and asked if my aunt had taken a turn for the worse.

"Er . . . no . . . no . . . she's fine . . . everything's fine," I lied. "I'm really looking forward to the weekend."

"Me too!" grinned Kate. "I've plans, you know. Big plans. I just know everything's going to work out brilliantly."

At that point I didn't really share her confidence, but I've got to admit that by eight o'clock that evening I was beginning to unwind. Madeleine and Maurice, Kate's parents, were nice – a bit odd, but definitely nice. They do everything by computer. As soon as I arrived Madeleine keyed in a list of my favourite foods so that the computer could tell Maurice what to cook for tea. Stuffed mackerel with orange and parsley followed by pear Belle Helene was what came up on the screen, which knocked my faith in computers rather as I'd said my favourite food was fish and chips and I loathe pears. I needn't have worried, though. When Maurice came home he fiddled around at the keyboard for a few minutes and then decided he didn't feel like cooking after all so we got four fish suppers from the chippy. I began to relax.

But the nice, comfortable feeling didn't last long. At half past eight Kate announced she had to make a phone call. After she'd been gone a couple of minutes Maurice went into the kitchen and left the door open. What I overheard from the hallway almost had me stuffing my A-ha nightshirt back into Mum's overnight case and catching the next bus home. Kate was speaking in a dramatic whisper – presumably to one of the music crowd: "Yes, Sarah's here. She doesn't suspect a thing. I can't wait to see what happens tomorrow!"

I suppose it was a mixture of embarrassment and pure curiosity that kept me glued to my bean-bag. "What don't I suspect?" I kept wondering, but I didn't like to ask. I mean, when Kate came back she was so friendly and such good fun I began to think I'd misheard. But the mystery of it all kept me awake until well after midnight, and when eventually I did drop off I had a horrible nightmare about disco dancing on the hockey pitch with the music crowd. They were sniggering behind my back. "She doesn't suspect a thing," Kate hissed and suddenly they all screeched with laughter. I woke up with my fingers in my ears trying to block out the sound. Screech . . . Screech . . . Screech . . . on and on it went, and then I realized it wasn't laughter. Someone – it had to be Kate – was playing a violin directly below me in the lounge. At 7.30 am!

"I always get up early to practise on Saturdays," she explained over breakfast. (The computer had recommended fresh orange juice, wholemeal bread and muesli; but we went for coffee and doughnuts.)

"I usually roll out of bed around eleven," I said, licking sugar from my upper lip.

"Oh dear, got you up a bit early then, didn't I?"

"S'all right," I said, and actually I meant it. There was something relaxing about sitting in the kitchen chatting to Kate. She'd even confided that she was scared stiff of the Youth Orchestra conductor, Mr Witherspoon (or Withers, as she called him). That was why she got up at the crack of dawn to practise.

"You see, secretly, I *dread* rehearsals," she said. This came as such a surprise I completely forgot about the phone call and the nightmare. I'd never imagined Kate dreading anyone or anything and suddenly I felt perfectly at ease with her . . . so when she asked in her most friendly manner if I'd like to come along to the orchestra, I bit

happily into my second (or was it my third?) doughnut and said, "Why not?"

Half an hour later, still feeling warm and comfortable, I trotted into my first ever orchestra rehearsal. "What a gruesome way to spend a Saturday morning," I thought, as my ears were blasted by a cat's chorus of instruments. And then I saw exactly what Kate had been talking about. A little man with a shock of red hair was standing with his back to us on a podium, exploding. Kate caught my eye and winked: "Yeah, that's him. Like a stick of gelignite, isn't he? Wonder what's set him off this time?"

I didn't even want to find out. "Er . . . Kate . . ." I muttered, "if it's all right by you, I think I'll wait in McDonald's."

A strange look passed over

Kate's face. "Oh but that would ruin everything!" She grasped me firmly by the arm. "You're here to be introduced."

"Introduced? Who to? No, please, not to Withers! Please, please stop, Kate!" My protests were useless. Kate was marching me to the podium, where, before my horrified eyes, she tapped Withers on the shoulder.

He spun round. Argh! I expected her to be electrocuted on the spot. "Yes, girl, what is it?"

Cool as an ice lolly Kate replied: "I've brought a new member of the percussion section to meet you. She's called Sarah."

A new member of the percussion section? Me! "No I'm not," I wailed.

"My dear," Withers lit up like a set of traffic lights, "I don't mind what you call yourself, though it seems to me that Sarah is as good a name as any. The important thing is that you have come at precisely the right moment. I have just heard that Tracy, our cymbal player, has left the area. I'm delighted to be able to replace her so promptly."

Even as he spoke everything slotted into place. Suddenly I knew what I hadn't suspected. Kate Forbes and the music crowd had set this up between them so they could have one great big laugh at my expense. They wanted me to squirm under the lash of Wither's tongue . . . to hear my mistakes and watch me desperately trying to wriggle out of the percussion section. I was so mad I forgot all about having short legs and not being able to play the recorder. I'd show them!

Round the back of the cat's chorus I went, past the trumpets and oboes, to where a guy who looked like a cross between Bobby Ewing and Bono was lounging behind a pair of kettle drums, smiling a really friendly sort of smile. "It just shows you can't judge by appearances," I thought darkly. He was one of the music crowd – probably the one Kate had been conspiring with on the phone.

"Hi, I'm Mike," he said.

"I'm here to play the cymbals," I snapped.

"Great," he said, handing them to me. "I mean it's really great you're here. Just slip your hands through the leather bits. Oops! That's the way. You'll soon get the knack. Now, how does it feel?"

"Stupid," I said. "What am I meant to do?"

"Watch Withers, keep counting and every time you see a sign like that," he pointed to the music, "bang 'em together as hard as you can."

Some things are easier said than done, and believe me, playing the cymbals is one of them. If I hadn't been so mad with Kate and Mike and Withers and the whole stupid music crowd I'd have given up after the first five minutes. As it was, I hung in, counting furiously, managing once in a while to produce a feeble tap at more or less the right moment. Every time I tapped Mike whispered "great stuff" in an encouraging tone which made me madder than ever.

"We'll finish with the *War March of the Priests*," said Withers, after one and a half hours of torture. "Cymbals, give it all you've got."

It was my last chance and I knew it. I'm not quite sure how it happened but at that moment everything came together; my mood, the music and most importantly, the cymbals. CRASH CRASH CRASH! I drowned every other instrument in the orchestra including Mike's drums and Kate's violin. Withers absolutely beamed at me over their heads. CRASH CRASH CRASH! Those priests sounded like a herd of elephants. CRASH CRASH CRASH CRASH! I was magnificent!

"BRILLIANT!" said Mike. It was over. The last CRASH died away and I laid down my cymbals. My hands were shaking and I was back to my normal size. "Brilliant," repeated Mike, "come on, we'll join the crowd for coffee."

For the first time I looked him straight in his good-looking, deceptively friendly face. He was smiling, and if I hadn't known better, I might have gone weak at the knees. "How can someone who seems so nice play such a dirty trick? I suppose Kate put him up to it," I thought bitterly. Out loud I said: "No thanks. I'm off home." And I bolted out of the hall.

Halfway across the car park I heard Kate's voice. "Stop, Sarah! Hold on a minute!" I broke into a run, but she soon caught up. (No prizes for guessing why!)

Dragging me down beside her onto a bench she panted, "Give me a chance to explain, would you?

That cymbals business wasn't meant to happen."

"Sure," I said. "And next year I'm going to win the Eurovision Song Contest! I heard you on the phone last night, Kate Forbes. 'She doesn't suspect a thing,' you said, and you were dead right – I didn't. But I'll be as suspicious as murder from now on. You and your sneaky friends won't get any more laughs at my expense."

"We weren't laughing, honest Sarah. We hadn't a clue you'd be landed with the cymbals. All we planned was for you to sit behind the kettle drums with Mike and hold his music or something. It just seemed like a good way of bringing you together."

"Of bringing us together?" I echoed faintly. And, do you know, the words gave me the oddest sensation – as if my legs were growing.

I don't know how long we sat on the bench after that. It was long enough for Kate to explain how she and the girls from the music crowd had been messing about with the computer, doing some computer dating and my name had come up on the screen linked with Mike's. "According to the computer you're made for each other," she replied. "If only things had gone the way I planned . . ."

And just at that moment who should come pedalling along, like a little ginger gnome on his bicycle, but Withers. "Well done, whoever you are," he yelled at me. "See you next week."

My legs grew another two inches, I remembered Mike's smile and made up my mind. "See you," I yelled back.

That was two days ago. You might say I'm one of the music crowd now. I knocked about with them all weekend and got on fantastically, especially with Mike. When Kate told her folks about us, Madeleine laughed her head off and said the computer had made a sensible suggestion at last. But Mike said technology had nothing to do with it. "It was the way you slammed those cymbals together and raised the roof," he told me. "You've a brilliant personality, Sarah." A brilliant personality – those were his words. And do you know, when I think back over what happened, I can't help feeling he's right!

Did you know the second most popular hobby in the UK is chess? For any Guide who enjoys this particular pastime, here's an idea to help you share your enthusiasm with the rest of your Company and, at the same time, have lots of fun.

Why not turn your Unit into a life-size chess set?

Chess has been around for 1400 years but the pieces and rules have developed in step with changes in society.

It's been played on the ground, on cloths and has represented the hierarchy of an army as well as courts.

The Queen, now the strongest piece in the game, started out as a weak man, 'Firz', a counsellor to the ruler. Having changed gender the piece today, particularly in countries without a monarchy, is called simply 'Lady'.

Chess pieces can be simple or intricately carved, small travelling sets to garden chess sets, with pieces so large they need two people to lift each one, and every possible variation in between.

You can tell a lot about chess pieces by their characteristics.

Pawn meant 'foot-soldier' in Arabic, so it's of the smallest size and value, slow, easily blocked, and it can't retreat.

The Knight represents the cavalry, and so it can attack any of up to eight squares and jump over other pieces.

So, for a special occasion, why not bring your game into 1989 and turn each Guide into a chess piece? A large Company will be able to make up both teams, but smaller Units could challenge another Company, or invite the local Rangers, Young Leaders or Scouts to join in.

Planning

Is this to be a display game, competition or drama workshop?

Do you need to involve other people?

How many already know how to play chess?

What's the best way for the others to learn?

What style of chess pieces do you want to be?

e.g. King Arthur's Court vs Robin Hood & his merry men.
Oliver Twist characters vs *EastEnders*.

Characters – how will your chosen theme fit with the chess characters? Nancy from *Oliver Twist* is an obvious choice for Queen, but who should be King – Fagin or Bill Sykes?

Costumes – will you put everyone in full costume, just use name labels or hats, or carry an item to show who you are? How would you represent Den or Michelle from *EastEnders*? A pub sign and a baby perhaps?

The game – who will represent each piece and who will be 'players', deciding when and where each piece should move?

Where will you play and how will the board be marked out?

Where can the 'players' stand so that they have a good view of the board?

Do you need a commentator?

How will you keep the game and the pieces moving?

What will the captured pieces do?

It's your move next!

For more information about chess, contact the British Chess Federation which manages and develops chess activities in this country and represents the UK in all international events.

The General Secretary
British Chess Federation
9a Grand Parade
St Leonards-on-Sea
EAST SUSSEX
TN38 0DD

by Pauline Ashton
illustrations Clive Goodyer

Helping children GROW!

Being healthy and happy are an important part of life and Guiding. But in many countries, good health is not just a matter of brushing teeth or doing aerobics – it can mean life or death for small children. **Robert Thomson**, *who works with UNICEF at the World Bureau, tells us more about how Girl Guides, Girl Scouts and Scouts around the world lend a hand to save a life!*

Every week, Mary Grace Mjoro walks to her Guide Company meeting in Mtendere village near the capital city of Zambia. She's fifteen, but has already helped save many children from suffering and possible death.

Mary Grace has learnt how to lay water pipes, and with thirty other Guides, helped bring a drinking water supply to the village market place.

As the Guides walk to their meetings, sometimes as far as eight kilometres on foot, they often call on families with small children. They chat with mothers and children, who say how good it is to have the water pipe in the market place, and explain to busy mothers the importance of using clean water.

Why is it so important? Many of the illnesses which affect children in the village are carried in water which is not properly purified. Water from streams and ponds, often much closer to homes than the piped supply, is infected with germs which attack the body and cause diarrhoea and vomiting.

Anyone who's been to camp can tell you how uncomfortable diarrhoea and vomiting can be! It can be cured very simply at camp, but did you know it causes the death of tens of thousands of babies and small children *every day*?

As you might have guessed, there's a huge difference between the health care projects overseas Guides take part in and the first-aid work we do in the UK.

Girl Guides in Zambia, and in places as far apart as Peru, Egypt and Sri Lanka, have studied the causes of diarrhoea and know how to prevent it.

The simplest and most natural way to prevent this deadly problem is to breastfeed babies for as long as possible. Mother's milk contains all the nourishment a new-born baby needs, and is not contaminated by the organisms found in ponds. To help spread this message, Guides in neighbouring Zimbabwe make posters encouraging breastfeeding and display them everywhere!

Another way is to make sure that babies and small children are well-nourished, clean and properly clothed. In Pakistan, Guides visit villages with posters, songs and shows about the importance of a balanced diet, and how to grow vegetables. The Homemaker badge can be a lifesaver!

Mary Grace's story

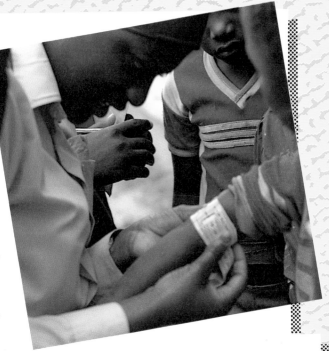

"Mothers enjoy listening to Guides talking about health, and really want to learn how to keep their children well. Diarrhoea and vomiting are a huge problem. It is very sad when a beautiful baby dies from such a simple illness. They lose energy and dry up, just like a cut flower in an empty vase, and sometimes mothers just don't know what to do. That's why we've learnt about a special drink to get water back into babies suffering from 'dehydration' – the drying up of the body which follows an attack of diarrhoea. The special drink was taught to our Guide Company by the people from UNICEF, who showed us how easy it is to make and how easy it is to save a life."

What UNICEF had to say

Girl Guides, Girl Scouts and Scouts around the world have been learning about Oral Rehydration Therapy (ORT) and also about immunization. These are simple remedies which everyone should know about.

Diarrhoea takes away the appetite, stops you absorbing food, burns up calories, drains away nutrients and leads to malnutrition. If parents knew the importance of continuing to feed their child plenty of food and fluids – instead of withholding them as they often mistakenly do – the health of millions of children could be improved.

Dehydration caused by diarrhoea is the most common cause of death among children in the poorest parts of the world. However, a simple solution of salt, sugar and water is enough to stop the dehydration process – saving 5 million lives a year.

Several countries have developed their own formula for ORT, using rice water, or other cereal products, fruit sugars and juices. Various homemade recipes for the solution are promoted throughout the world. At the same time, prepacked sachets are becoming more widely available.

The Do-it-yourself Recipe
1 Use clean utensils and wash hands.
2 Boil one litre of clean water and let it cool.
3 Add to the water:
 a ¼ teaspoon of salt
 b ¼ teaspoon baking soda (bicarbonate of soda)
  (If you have no soda, add another ¼ teaspoon of salt.)
 c Two tablespoons of sugar or honey.

Stir the solution well. Before giving the drink, taste it. It should not taste more salty than tears.

You may add half a cup of orange juice or coconut milk or a little mashed ripe banana. The person with diarrhoea should be given frequent drinks until the stools return to normal.

Mary Grace has a pen-friend in Uganda, which is north of Zambia up Lake Tanganyika. In Uganda, Guides and Scouts are helping UNICEF and the Ministry of Health to immunize babies and children in Kampala, the capital city.

Many children die and many others are mentally or physically disabled by six diseases – even though there are vaccines to prevent them. The six diseases are measles, whooping cough, tetanus, poliomyelitis, diphtheria and tuberculosis. Most kids in Britain are immunized against them, but in Africa, Asia and Latin America there's still lots of work to be done.

Recently, Mary Grace's friend wrote to her about what she was doing to protect children against these killer diseases.

Dear Mary Grace,

I really enjoyed meeting you at the African regional gathering for Guides, and taking part in your project in Ntendere. The UNICEF people were very helpful – in fact since they spoke to us, Guides and Scouts in Uganda have been busy helping to get children immunized. I thought I'd tell you all about what we've learnt and what we are doing.

Measles is a very common disease and you know how easily one child can catch it from another. It's so sad to see them catch what looks like a bad cold, and then watch it turn to fever with red spots on the face and body. My mother said it was just a normal part of growing up! But I've learnt that it's a very dangerous, even deadly disease, especially when babies are hungry and weak because of malnutrition. When they are weak they catch more diseases, like pneumonia, or diarrhoea. I explained all this to my mum and she was so shocked that we decided to tell all the mothers in our neighbourhood.

Each Guide and Scout made posters about measles and the other diseases. We found out where the immunization clinic was, and the times and days when they immunize children. The vaccine comes from a big warehouse near the airport, and the delivery is made every few days in a lorry with a refrigerator on the back to keep the vaccine cool.

We now go around the neighbourhood, visiting homes to explain why it is so important to vaccinate children. We also tell parents not to worry if the baby cries all night after a visit to the clinic, it's just their bodies getting used to the vaccine. It's very hard work, but worthwhile to watch children grow up so healthy!

Oh by the way, we have a special badge to go on our Guide uniform, and I thought you'd like one.

Hope to see you again soon!

Yedi Nabajja

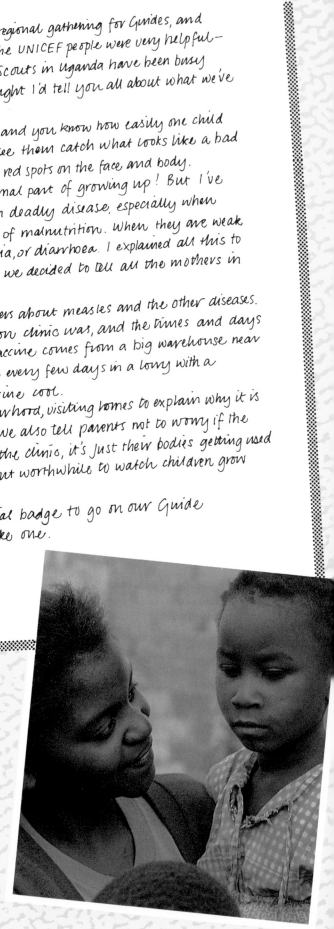

There are hundreds of thousands of young people overseas like Mary Grace and Yedi, who are putting into action the Guide Promise. But even with over 25 million Girl Guides, Girl Scouts and Scouts joining in, the struggle to give health to all children is not over. Lots more has to be done – and you can help. Try discussing the subject with other Guides or school friends; find out how you can support these projects; write to UNICEF or WAGGGS for more information; get a pen-friend yourself in a developing country by writing to the Postbox Secretary, c/o International Department, CHQ. But above all, enter our competition if you want to learn more about Guiding in developing countries.

Enny and Aban

My name's Enny. I knew something was wrong the minute I picked up my little brother Aban from the bed. He was burning with fever, his eyes looked red and watery, and he was whimpering in a sad way in between dry little coughs. He'd suddenly changed from the happy one-year-old I used to play with and look after every day.

Before leaving for the market that morning, Mother had said, "Please look after Aban while I'm gone, Enny. You know he's had a cold for the past few days; well he's still asleep. The rest will do him good – he'll probably feel better when he wakes up."

But I was worried. It was clear that Aban wasn't any better. As I gazed at him, I noticed a red-spotted rash starting to break out on his skin. I was scared. I'd heard Mother and the other women in the village talking about children in the town who were sick like this. Some had even died.

I knew I had to do something for Aban quickly. But what? As it was market day, most of the other women in the village had gone with Mother into town to sell produce.

I wrapped Aban in a light blanket, carried him outside and hurried down the path to look for help. But I didn't really know where to go.

At the edge of the village I noticed some boys and girls, not much older than me, walking towards a cluster of houses. They wore identical scarves around their necks and they carried pencils and boards covered in papers. I think I remember my older sister chatting about these people . . . Scouts or Guides, I think she called them. She was really keen to join them, that was for sure.

They come from a village near ours, but I've seen them over here quite a few times recently; talking to people about their children. They were trying to find out how often children are sick, what kinds of sicknesses they get and how parents react to these illnesses.

"Maybe," I thought, "they could help Aban, or tell me where to go for help."

I walked towards the young people with the scarves. They smiled . . .

Competition

Why not finish the story of Enny and Aban? What happened to them after they met these people? What kind of help did they find? Did Aban recover and, if so, how is he doing now? What, if anything, changed for Enny, her parents and family, or the people in the village after this episode?

Illustrate your story, if possible, with your own drawings.

Do some more research into measles, send for information from WAGGGS or UNICEF. Has anyone in your area been to a developing country recently? Why not invite them to talk at a Company meeting about their experiences?

The prize for the best story? We've got five Thermos cool bags and vacuum flasks to give away. In countries like Uganda these play a vital role in the 'cold chain' from port to remote village, keeping the measles vaccine cool.

Win one for you or your Company, for camps, picnics or holidays.

Send your entries, no later than 31 March, 1989, to the Editor (address page 46).

WAGGGS,
World Bureau,
Olave Centre,
12c Lyndhurst Road,
London, NW3 5PQ.

UNICEF (UK),
55 Lincoln's Inn Fields
London, WC2A 3NB.

photographs Robert Thomson, Thermos

GET CRACKING!

by Julia Nellthorp
illustrations Nicola Heindl

Crackers have been around for over 100 years. In about 1840 Tom Smith, a London sweetshop owner, saw some sweets in Paris wrapped in paper twisted at both ends. He decided to copy the idea – and to improve upon it. He added love messages in the wraps and spent years developing a harmless strip of paper which would go 'Bang' when torn apart. Crackers were certainly not limited to Christmas treats for children in Victorian Britain and they were often brought out at dinner parties if a lull occurred in the conversation.

Nowadays we tend to associate crackers with Christmas, but why limit the fun to one occasion in the year? Crackers make all kinds of parties and celebrations go with a bang! And if you make your own they are even more special.

You will need for each basic cracker:

◆ a piece of single crêpe paper 30.5cm × 17cm with the grain running the length of the paper

◆ a piece of lining paper (tissue paper is good for this) 28cm × 15cm

◆ a snap (available from many craft shops)

◆ motto or message

◆ present or filling

◆ stiffening card 15cm × 9cm

◆ two pieces of plastic pipe or other suitable former. Both 3.7cm in diameter, one 25cm long and the other 12.5cm long

◆ non-toxic glue

◆ strong string

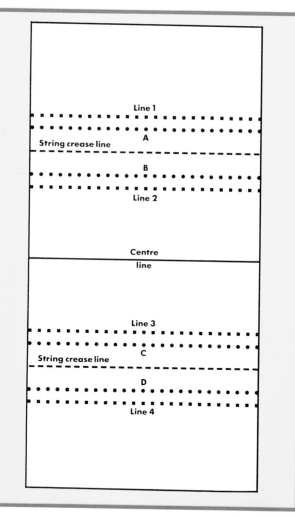

How to make the basic cracker

1 *Transfer the plan to a piece of card. The measurements must be accurate. Lay the crêpe paper on the plan, then place the lining paper, snap and motto on top. Lay the stiffening card in line with lines 2 and 3 on the plan.*

2 *Spread a thin layer of glue along the crêpe paper, visible at the top edge. Put the longest piece of tubing on the card. Then put the other pipe on the paper to form a continuous tube.*

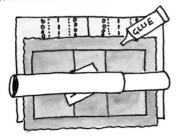

3 *Roll the crêpe paper over the tubes starting with the edge nearest you. Make sure you roll quite tightly and keep the two tubes in line. Press down firmly on the glued edge.*

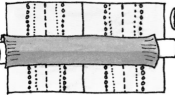

4 *Feel for the join in the shaping tubes and line this up with line C on the plan. Ease the short tube gently away from the longer one until it sits on line D.*

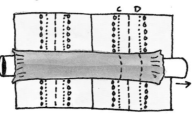

5 *Put a piece of string around the cracker along the string line. Pull tight. Push the tubes back together again and give them a slight twist to even up the neck. Take off the string and take out the shorter piece of tube.* DON'T LET THE LONGER PIECE OF TUBE COME OUT.

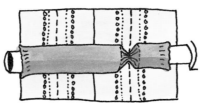

6 *Put the present into the open end and then lay the cracker back on the plan. Slide the shaping tube until it reaches line A. Tie the neck with the string as before, then remove the shaping tube.*

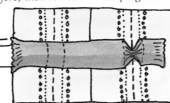

Your basic cracker is now complete!

CREPE   LINING   CARD   PLAN

Fillings

You can really let your imagination run riot with fillings. The only limiting factor is the small space!

Here are just a few ideas:
Tiny bars of soap, pieces of ribbon or lace, badges, bookmarks, sweets, marbles, chocolate coins, small sachets of herbs or spices, earrings, thimbles, small toys, pencil sharpeners, set of jacks, dice . . .

Decorations

Now you've got a basic cracker, use your artistic skills to decorate it. Stick some dried or fabric flowers, ribbons, Christmas baubles, lace, seeds, feathers, shells, beads, or tinsel on the crackers. Or go back to the Victorian-style, use appropriate pictures from magazines or even dig out some funny photographs of the guests as babies and see who can recognise who! To make the crackers personal you could try your hand at calligraphy and create some name or initial labels. Personalising the crackers is useful if you've put special presents for each guest inside.

Once you've mastered the art of making crackers using crêpe paper (the easiest to handle), experiment with different patterned papers. Try wrapping paper, wallpaper, tissue paper or even sheets of old magazines or newspapers if finances are tight! Do remember that crackers have to be pulled apart so don't use anything too sturdy!

Hit the street

Street theatre is exciting, colourful, spontaneous and inventive. It doesn't need a theatre building, props or costumes, so it can be performed almost anywhere and, if it's good enough, will always draw an audience, who are usually asked to join in too!

by Kate Simon
photographs | Noellec, Gareth Roberts

Street theatre's been around for centuries. You can find mime artists in Roman art and literature, and one of the greatest influences on street theatre today is the *commedia dell'arte* who entertained during the 16th to 18th centuries. They acted out humorous scenes using stock characters, lots of masks, jokes and mime. Characters such as Harlequin or Punchinello (alias Mr Punch) all come from this tradition, as does pantomime.

In the last decade street theatre has become big business. It's become so popular that some of the best performers have left the street for the fame, fortune and comfortable surroundings of the alternative clubs. Television and radio have got in on the act, with successful programmes like Channel 4's *Saturday Night Live*. And stars such as Rik Mayall, Dawn French and many famous actors, have all made it big from such humble roots.

'You have to be totally dedicated,' one artist told me. 'If you're not or you think you can hold down a full-time job and just work on the streets at weekends, you'll never get anywhere. There are too many people out there already working flat out for success.'

The most popular acts have always been magicians, jugglers, mime artists, escapologists and musicians, and you can guarantee seeing one or more of these acts if you visit any street theatre venue.

Take one fine Saturday afternoon in perhaps the UK's most famous street theatre venue, Covent Garden. There are a variety of acts to see on the two legitimate pitches (areas which performers are legally allowed to use) and plenty of busking too in the side streets.

In the West Piazza, I came across Zander the Wimp's act drawing to its climax. Zander is a comic escapologist. Dressed in a leopard skin costume which would look more at home on Tarzan, Zander is being tied up with chains and padlocks by two members of the audience. When the job is completed he announces to a captivated crowd that he will free himself in just three minutes.

The clock starts but Zander seems unruffled. He walks about the crowd chatting to people, until with a minute to go he suddenly rushes back to the street stage in a frenzy, desperately trying to free himself from his chains. He finally succeeds with just seconds to spare.

People show their appreciation by putting money into his hat during the act. Contributions aren't compulsory but most people I spoke to said this was a real way to support street theatre and show they'd enjoyed the performance.

Nebular, a male and female mime group, have meanwhile started their act. Mime has recently been popularised thanks to bodypopping, breakdancing and robotics. Nebular are professionally trained and today their sketches include a sequence to a record sung by Lady Penelope and Parker of Thunderbirds fame, a take-off of Michael Jackson's *Thriller* video, and an Avengers-style tale of a cat burglar foiled by his lady victim.

Another act has begun over in the West Piazza; a juggler is amazing onlookers with his skills, but the act takes a comic turn at its climax when he lights up three fire torches. Up to now the juggler has been following an instruction book, set on a stand. Juggling with fire adds drama to the act, but our supposedly novice juggler begins to drop his props and sets his clothes and the instruction book on fire! This may sound dangerous but it's all carefully rehearsed and the audience are kept well away from the action.

Getting the audience involved is a key part of many street performers' acts. Take The Officials. Dressed in medieval costume they explain to the audience that a damsel in distress is needed and proceed to drag the unlikely candidate – a moustached man – from the crowd, dress him in a large cone hat, a veil and a skirt, and tie him to one of the church pillars. Here he remains until the end of the act – a fight between the two men to rescue the 'damsel'. During this time he's the object of a mock knife throwing act among other 'tortures', and the scorer in a fencing duel.

Most people who've been through this terrifying ordeal usually say how nervous and silly they felt at first but how much fun it seemed afterwards to be so involved. Every one in the audience enjoyed the performances. One woman told me she'd brought her children to see street theatre because she thought it was as important as a visit to the Science Museum! Lots of others agreed they'd go out of their way to see more!

You can find street theatre almost anywhere in the UK where there's a suitable venue and often in places where there isn't! Summer fêtes, village fairs, community theatre festivals and local markets are the obvious places to look. Although street performers can only legally perform on legitimate pitches, you may also find them in tube stations, on trains or even in shop windows. There are also special events like the Bath, Edinburgh or Brighton Festivals which play host to street theatre, and the Fringe festival at Edinburgh is well worth a visit if you have the chance. Find out about events in your area by contacting your regional arts association – the addresses are given below. They might also be able to tell you how to get involved yourself. In many towns you'll be able to find workshops teaching mime, juggling and breakdancing. Why not hassle your drama teacher to let you have a go?

Street theatre mustn't be allowed to disappear. In the end, only you and I can ensure that it survives by enjoying the experience, joining in, and supporting its right to be on the street, available for everyone.

For information about events in your area contact:

Eastern Arts
Cherry Hinton Hall
Cherry Hinton Road
Cambridge
CB1 4DW

Buckinghamshire Arts
55 High Street
Aylesbury
Buckinghamshire
HP20 1SA

Greater London Arts
9 White Lion Street
London
N1 9PD

Lincolnshire & Humberside Arts
St Hugh's
Newport
Lincoln
LN1 3DN

Merseyside Arts
Bluecoat Chambers
School Lane
Liverpool
L1 3BX

Northern Arts
9–10 Osborne Terrace
Newcastle upon Tyne
NE2 1NZ

North West Arts
12 Harter Street
Manchester
M1 6HY

Southern Arts
19 Southgate Street
Winchester
Hampshire
SO23 9DQ

South East Arts
10 Mount Ephraim
Tunbridge Wells
Kent
TN4 8AS

South West Arts
Bradnich Place
Gandy Street
Exeter
EX4 3LS

East Midlands Arts
Mountfields House
Forest Road
Loughborough
Leicestershire
LE11 3HU

West Midlands Arts
82 Granville Street
Birmingham
B1 2LH

Yorkshire Arts Association
Glyde House
Glydegate
Bradford
BD5 0BQ

What's underneath your TENT

When you're at camp, have you ever seriously considered what goes on underneath your tent – or anyone else's come to that? Before you plonk yourself down on the groundsheet, spare a thought for the creatures who live in the field your Company has commandeered for the week. Even the smallest area will be teeming with wildlife. Take a closer look – you may be surprised at what you find:

The humble earthworm, it has to be said, is not the field's most attractive resident. With few distinguishing features save its length and sliminess, the earthworm nevertheless is an important link in the food-chain. One of its most important jobs is to aerate the soil which benefits insects and plants alike, and it's a main meal for a blackbird or thrush. Keep an eye open after rain and you could see these birds out worm hunting, as worms move towards the surface during wet weather.

There will probably be ants underneath your tent, but don't worry they'll be too busy to bother you. Ants live in permanent communities with a whole army of workers foraging for food and doing the chores to relieve the queen of any cares. She spends her days in a 'brood chamber' laying eggs and rearing more and more young.

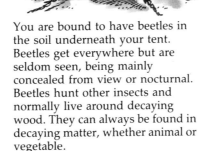

You are bound to have beetles in the soil underneath your tent. Beetles get everywhere but are seldom seen, being mainly concealed from view or nocturnal. Beetles hunt other insects and normally live around decaying wood. They can always be found in decaying matter, whether animal or vegetable.

Moles are well known for their tunnelling abilities and the distinctive hills they make. There shouldn't be much chance of putting up your tent on a mole hill as they are fairly obvious! But if there are some in the area there could be tunnels running underneath your tent. You won't be bothered by the moles themselves, you'll just have lots of activity beneath your sleeping bag!

Strictly speaking you're unlikely to get grasshoppers underneath your tent (they'll have the sense to move!) but you could well have plenty around the tent. There are two kinds of grasshopper – short-horned and long-horned. Short-horned grasshoppers are the noisiest and the volume of their 'song' is in direct response to heat and sunshine, so they'll be at their noisiest on a hot summer day.

Rabbits and badgers live underground but unless something has gone wrong with your Guider's planning, you won't have rabbits or badgers underneath your tent, as their warrens and sets are usually in the more remote parts of the countryside. What you might be able to do is to go badger or rabbit-watching. Badgers are particularly shy and only hunt at night, so you'll need to be very patient. The warden of the camp site will know which animals are regular visitors to the site, and if there are any which can be watched at close quarters. He or she may organise animal watches. Rabbits in particular are out and about in the early mornings, just after dawn.

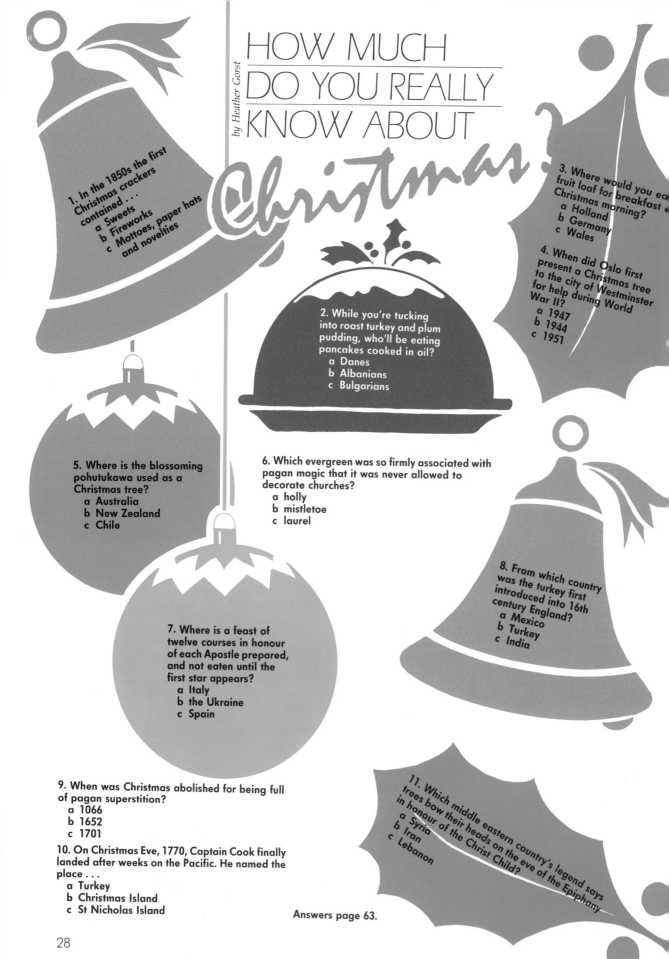

HOW MUCH DO YOU REALLY KNOW ABOUT

by Heather Gorst

Christmas?

1. In the 1850s the first Christmas crackers contained . . .
 a Sweets
 b Fireworks
 c Mottoes, paper hats and novelties

2. While you're tucking into roast turkey and plum pudding, who'll be eating pancakes cooked in oil?
 a Danes
 b Albanians
 c Bulgarians

3. Where would you eat fruit loaf for breakfast Christmas morning?
 a Holland
 b Germany
 c Wales

4. When did Oslo first present a Christmas tree to the city of Westminster for help during World War II?
 a 1947
 b 1944
 c 1951

5. Where is the blossoming pohutukawa used as a Christmas tree?
 a Australia
 b New Zealand
 c Chile

6. Which evergreen was so firmly associated with pagan magic that it was never allowed to decorate churches?
 a holly
 b mistletoe
 c laurel

7. Where is a feast of twelve courses in honour of each Apostle prepared, and not eaten until the first star appears?
 a Italy
 b the Ukraine
 c Spain

8. From which country was the turkey first introduced into 16th century England?
 a Mexico
 b Turkey
 c India

9. When was Christmas abolished for being full of pagan superstition?
 a 1066
 b 1652
 c 1701

10. On Christmas Eve, 1770, Captain Cook finally landed after weeks on the Pacific. He named the place . . .
 a Turkey
 b Christmas Island
 c St Nicholas Island

11. Which middle eastern country's legend says trees bow their heads on the eve of the Epiphany in honour of the Christ Child?
 a Syria
 b Iran
 c Lebanon

Answers page 63.

Why spiders climb so fast

Amabel Williams-Ellis

illustrations Jill Gibbon

Anansi!
You people all know about Anansi? And how sometimes he's a man, sometimes he's a great big spider. But always he's trying to cheat other people and boast!

Now one day this Anansi was walking along the path and saw a breadfruit tree. Well, that isn't anything special! I know that, but Anansi saw that, on the very last end of the longest branch of this breadfruit tree, there's a big, big breadfruit! All nice and ripe it was, and hanging over the hard path, just where it might fall upon a stone and get all mashed up. Anansi thinks how to get this breadfruit, and he thinks he can't do it all himself because if he climbs out on the branch and cuts the breadfruit then, for sure, it will fall on the path! On the stones! And get

all mashed up! And that won't do.

He must find someone to help him. Because, you see, how can he shake the branch and catch the breadfruit at the same time? That's what he calculated.

So Anansi sat down by the path and he waited.

By and by there is someone coming along the path. Who? Oh, it's a beetle, you know, a stumble-toddler. What's that? Well, that's the sort of beetle that packs up a little ball of dung and he rolls his little ball into his hole. That's how a stumble-toddler lives! This stumble-toddler was rolling a nice ball of dung this morning.

Anansi got up and said, 'Good morning, Master Stumble-Toddler.'

And Stumble-Toddler said, 'Good morning, Anansi.' But Stumble-Toddler said that in a very

busy voice, and he went on rolling his little ball of dung.

Anansi said all pitiful, 'Oh, Master Stumble-Toddler, please – I beg you – come and help me!'

So then he told Stumble-Toddler how he couldn't get the breadfruit alone, or else it would fall on stones – and get all mashed up. Stumble-Toddler didn't answer, not one word, he just went on rolling his ball down the path.

Anansi ran alongside him and he begged, 'You come for me, oh, do please! You help me?'

Stumble-Toddler only said, 'Nonsense!' in a deep voice, 'I've got no time to spare!' And he just wouldn't stop, he went on rolling his ball of dung till he'd rolled it down into his hole and he went down after it.

So Anansi was all alone again. And he sat down to wait. By and by Anansi saw another gentleman coming. This was Master Tomcat. Anansi got up and he made a low bow, and he said, 'Good morning, Brother Tomcat, dear Master Tomcat! Nice Tomcat! You're just the man I love to see!'

Master Tomcat only said, 'Miaow! What do you waaant, Anansi?' (But he did trot up a bit nearer.)

'Oh Master Tomcat, good Master Tomcat, would you please catch this breadfruit for me when I climb up the tree and shake the bough?'

Cat said, 'Miaow! Can't be bothered! You want breadfruit, you get it yourself! I don't *like* breadfruit.'

Anansi begged him, 'Oh, kind Master Tomcat, Godfather Tomcat!'

'Miaow! No time to spare!'

Anansi was very vexed, 'Tomcat, you're a worthless fellow! You're nothing but a lazy fellow! You're the one that only eats rats instead of pork and beef!'

Cat didn't care one least bit what names Anansi called him, just shook his ears and trotted off down the path.

Anansi sat down again. He waited a long time – ten minutes. Then he saw someone else coming down the path. It was Dog.

Anansi called out, 'Oh, Master Dog, you're just such a nice gentleman!'

Dog said, 'Wow, wow!' (But he did wag his tail.)

'Oh, Master Dog, do you know who it is speaking? It's I, your brother Anansi, friend of all honourable dogs!' And then

Anansi explained what it was he wanted Dog to do.

Dog looked up and Dog barked, 'Yes, yes, yes!'

Anansi was so pleased he's dancing up and down.

'Oh, there's a real gentleman! The gentleman for me! Stay right there!'

So Dog stayed right there, and Anansi ran quickly and he climbed up the breadfruit tree, and he jumped bang! flump! on to the branch, and he jumped up and down on that branch. But, oh dear, nothing dropped down except leaves. And they dropped down on Dog's face.

Dog called out, 'Aw! Aw! Aw!!!'

Anansi called down through the tree, 'I can't understand what you're saying, Master Dog. Do show me what you mean?'

'Oh, Anansi, I want my eyes,' says Dog. But Anansi only jumped on the branch again, like that, to shake it again – hard.

This time the big breadfruit *did* drop and Dog caught it in his mouth. Anansi called down, 'Oh, clever Mr Dog! Oh, good Mr Dog. Hold it, hold it till I come! Don't squeeze! Don't squeeze!'

Dog's mouth was full with breadfruit so he didn't say anything. Anansi ran down the tree, fast, but before he could get down, Dog had started to run fast, fast down the path with the big ripe breadfruit in his mouth. Anansi was yelling out, 'Stop! Stop! Dog! Dog! Do! Do! Nice honourable gentleman!'

Dog didn't stop. Dog ran down the path and right out of Anansi's sight. Anansi was running too. By and by Dog got so far ahead that Anansi couldn't see where he had gone. But Anansi ran on, thinking soon he'd surely get to the very spot where Dog was?

That was true enough, only, you see, Dog knew where there was a big hole right by the side of the path, big enough for him, and big enough for the breadfruit in his mouth as well. And before Anansi could get there, Dog had whipped down that hole quick.

So now you understand! Dog's in the hole with the breadfruit behind him, and Dog's looking back up out of the hole at Anansi, and Anansi couldn't see him. Dog had just gone! Anansi looked up. No, Dog wasn't in the sky. And Dog wasn't in the trees. Dog had just gone! So Anansi stood there wondering and

pondering, and pondering and wondering. At last he looked down. And so at last he saw two big eyes looking up at him out of the ground.

But Anansi couldn't think what that was. Anansi was never so surprised!

'Oh!' he called out. 'What's that?'

But Dog didn't say anything at all, just looked, and looked, and looked. Then Anansi remembered a proverb. The proverb was: WALLS HAVE EARS, AND RIVERS HAVE MOUTHS. That's true enough, thought Anansi, but I never heard before that GROUND HAS EYES.

And Anansi never knew that that was only Dog looking up at him.

But, you know, Anansi wasn't one to waste anything, and he thought to himself, 'If I never heard that GROUND HAS EYES, perhaps other people don't know that either? The breadfruit – that's gone! Perhaps instead there's a meal in this for me?'

Well, when Anansi felt sure he'd got a real big piece of news – something that *never*, anybody, had ever heard tell before – he begin to think he's a big important man!

'Oh, if only me can tell that to the biggest man of them all – to the General. That General, he ought to know that "Ground Has Eyes", and me – Anansi – is the one to tell him!'

So Anansi ran fast, fast, to the camp where the soldiers and officers and the General were. I don't know why, but there wasn't any sentry soldier down there at the camp gate that day, or was it because Anansi not bother with gates? Anyhow, Anansi just got into the camp.

A soldier came out and said in a gruff voice, 'What you want?'

'Ho, ho!' said Anansi, puffing himself out to look big, 'I'm Anansi, I got to see the General.'

The soldier went to fetch the corporal. The corporal said, 'What you want to see the General about?'

'Ho, ho,' said Anansi again, 'I'm Anansi! I got special news!'

Corporal fetched an officer, and Anansi told the officer the same thing. The officer listened to him and at last he said, 'All right, "Nancy".'

Just then it happened that the General came out. That General was a big man. Anansi admired him very much. Thinks: 'How grand to have dem big boots an' red

coat, an' hat with gold and feathers on it. Very grand.' Then Anansi said, 'Good evening, sir! Good evening, Master General. I'm Anansi, sir. I need to speak wid you. I need to tell you de big news.'

The General looked down at Anansi and then he said in his big voice, 'What is it now?'

Anansi looked up at the General and said, 'Sir, I seen a great thing down there! I always heard tell WALLS HAVE EARS AND RIVERS HAVE MOUTHS, but, sir, de news is de GROUND HAS EYES!'

'When did you see that, Anansi?' asked the General.

'Oh, just a while ago! Oh, sir! It's the greatest of all news!'

The General said, 'Well, it's certainly news to me.'

Anansi answered, 'Oh, come with me, sir! I show you right now, sir!'

General spoke again in his big voice, 'If I do come I shall bring the soldiers, but I shall make them shoot you if you've taken me on a fool's errand, and if we don't see that the Ground has got Eyes.'

'Oh, sir, you can bring the whole army!' said Anansi. 'I sure show dem!'

General said, 'Very well, but first I laugh at you and then I shoot you, if you don't let me see.'

'Oh, sir,' said Anansi, and he was still gazing up at the General, 'if anything it's I that will do the laughing!'

The General said, 'How far is it from here?'

'Oh, it's only five or twenty miles, sir.'

General looked down at Anansi and said in his deep voice, 'What do you mean by miles, you funny little "Nancy"? Do you mean feet?'

'Oh no, General – sir – I don't never mean feet! It's yards I mean when I say miles.'

Well, the General had decided a long time ago that he was going to have what they call manoeuvres – exercises. He was going out with his soldiers, and he thought he might as well go the way Anansi said, and see if what Anansi said was true.

So everything was fixed up, and it was a bargain; if the General came, and Anansi couldn't show that the Ground has Eyes, then he – the General – had got the right first to laugh, and then for the soldiers to shoot Anansi.

The General with his red coat got on his big white horse. Out he went with all his soldiers. Anansi was so excited!

'For me dis band is!' The band was playing loud – Rom – Tom – Tom! They'd got guns as well – bang – bang!

Anansi with his tiny feet, and the General with his horse and red coat and his big boots, and his hat with feathers, went first, and they all marched off; Anansi with his tiny feet had to run to march with the rest.

Anansi kept looking back and there were all the soldiers coming along after, and Anansi said, 'I'm de greatest man in the world! Some day I going to conquer dem all!'

Soon they came to the place where Dog had been hiding with the breadfruit in the hole.

Anansi said to the General, 'Sir General! Please tell de soldiers to halt!'

So the General told the officers and the sergeants shouted out 'Halt!' Then the General spoke to Anansi, 'Now, Anansi, you show me! If you can't, it isn't you that'll do the laughing.'

Then the General gave another order, and Anansi saw how all the soldiers were moving. They were moving so that they were all round him.

You've guessed what happened, oh my people? Yes, that's right! What had happened was that a long time ago, Dog had gone home and Mrs Dog – his wife – she'd cooked the breadfruit nicely for him and for the puppies. Dog wasn't there any more; that hole wasn't his place. He didn't live there with his wife and puppies!

But you see Anansi didn't know this, so when the General spoke he still felt proud and saluted just the way he'd seen the soldiers doing, and he answered the General, 'Yes, sir! Yes, sir!'

So Anansi went and looked at the sides of the road – up and down – with all his might. The General twiddled his moustache and he said in his big voice, 'Show me the eyes! Show me the eyes!'

Anansi was still looking and looking, but all he said was, 'Yes, sir, Yes, sir! But – but – please wait a minute!'

Well, Anansi went on looking; he was looking, but he couldn't see anything. So at last the General said he couldn't wait any longer. Anansi just said, 'Yes, sir!' once more, in a frightened voice this time.

Then the soldiers all started to laugh. 'Ho! ho! ho!' they laughed, and Anansi was afraid. Then they came all round, and Anansi could see that they were just getting ready to shoot.

'Please, sir!' called out Anansi. 'Please, kind Godfather General! Tell them to wait a minute!' Anansi was crying with big tears. 'Oh, sir, it's too hot here, please make them soldiers shoot me under that big tree there! Not here! I don't want to end my life when I'm too hot!'

The General nodded. He agreed to that. So Anansi got under the tree, and all the soldiers got ready to shoot, and the band played.

Then they shot, and there was a big noise! Boom, boom! Rattle, rattle! But dear me! Nothing fell – except some green leaves off the tree. Why? Because, you see, by the time the soldiers had all got ready, and they'd fired, Anansi was away up the tree – away up to the very very top!

So in the end it really was Anansi that did the laughing.

And that is why spiders climb so fast and why they like to live on the ceiling or at tops of trees. Ceiling Thomas – that's one of Anansi's names to this day.

The Story Spirits and Other Tales from Around the World, by Amabel Williams-Ellis is published by William Heinemann Ltd and this extract is reproduced here by kind permission of Dr Rachel Garden.

Caribbean
·CUISINE·

by Julia Nellthorp
illustrations Jill Gibbon

Starvation In De Market-Place

All kind o' breadfruit, pumpkin, potato and melon,
Banana, mango, paw-paw and lemon;
Men drinking beer and stout;
Children running all about;
Women licking off duh mout';
And I hungry luk a dog.

Glyne Walrond
from *The Children's Voice* (Stockwell)

Not many of us can actually visit the Caribbean but you can cook-up some of the sunshine and atmosphere with traditional Caribbean dishes. All of the recipes below are easy to prepare and you don't have to fly to Jamaica to buy the ingredients!

As you cook and eat, think of long palm-fringed beaches and calypso music playing gently in the background or the bustle of a Caribbean market place.

Babotee

227g cooked minced meat
1 chopped medium onion
1 egg
2 teaspoons butter
1 dessertspoon curry powder
1 finely-chopped red pepper
2 slices stale bread
a little milk
salt and pepper

Mix the meat with the chopped onion, pepper, seasonings, curry powder and the butter. Beat the egg and mix with the meat mixture. Soak the bread in cold water, squeeze dry, shred and add to the mixture with a little milk to moisten. Grease a small casserole and put the Babotee mixture in. Dot the top with butter and bake uncovered at 180°C (350°F, gas mark 4) for 20–30 minutes.

Calypso fish

28g plain flour
¼ teaspoon cayenne pepper
454g any white fish
57g butter
1 large onion, finely sliced
45ml white wine vinegar
¼ teaspoon cinnamon
¼ teaspoon ground mace
pinch of ground cloves
142ml cold water
1 teaspoon cornflour
2 teaspoons tomato puree
1 small green pepper – deseeded and cut into thin strips

Mix the flour, half the cayenne pepper and some salt and pepper together. Cut the fish into pieces approximately 75mm×50mm and lightly coat in the seasoned flour. Melt the butter in a large frying pan and cook the fish gently for 3–4 minutes on each side or until golden brown. Carefully remove from the pan and keep warm. Fry the onions until soft. Mix together the vinegar, cinnamon, mace and cloves and add to the frying pan. Keep the heat very low. Blend together the water and cornflour. Stir in the tomato puree and add to the frying pan. Stir in the green pepper and bring the sauce to the boil. Arrange the fish on a serving plate and pour the sauce over. If you can get sweet potatoes serve with these. If not, serve with saute potatoes and vegetables.

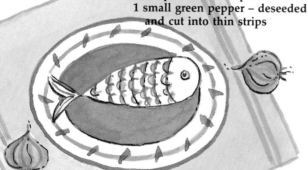

Red bean rice

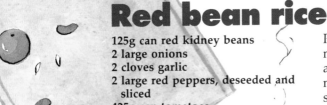

125g can red kidney beans
2 large onions
2 cloves garlic
2 large red peppers, deseeded and sliced
425g can tomatoes
150ml stock
225g rice
salt and pepper
3 teaspoons ground coriander
1 teaspoon chilli powder

Peel and chop the onions and fry gently for 10 minutes until they are tender. Stir in the garlic and red peppers and fry for a few more minutes. Add the can of tomatoes and the stock. Cook the rice with the spices and seasoning and leave to stand for 15 minutes once it is cooked. Add the bean mixture and stir gently. Check the seasoning and add more if necessary. Re-heat before serving.

This tastes delicious served with a green salad.

Roti

Stalls selling Roti are a common sight in the Caribbean, especially in Trinidad.

227g plain flour
pinch salt
½ teaspoon bicarbonate of soda
4–5 tablespoons milk
ghee

Prepare the ghee first. Put 57g butter in a cup and stand in hot water. When it has melted, pour off the oiled butter and throw away the sediment. To make the Roti sift the flour, bicarbonate of soda and salt, and bind with enough milk to make a stiff dough. Flour your hands and roll the dough into balls about the size of an egg. Flatten and spread with ghee, then pat back into the egg shape again. Flatten once more and cook in a hot frying pan turning frequently and brushing with ghee. Serve hot.

Baked bananas

30ml clear honey
2 tablespoons demerara sugar
½ teaspoon ground allspice
½ teaspoon ground cinnamon
285ml orange juice
1 tablespoon cornflour
4 bananas
1 orange

Blend together the orange juice and cornflour. Put into a saucepan with the honey, sugar and spices. Bring gently to the boil, stirring continuously. Peel the bananas and carefully make a slit along the length of each one. Pour over the sauce. Bake for 10–15 minutes at 180°C (350°F, gas mark 4). While the bananas are cooking, grate the rind of the orange and put to one side for decoration. Slice as much of the pith off as possible and cut the orange into segments. 5 minutes before the bananas are ready add the orange segments. Sprinkle some of the grated rind on top before serving.

Ragtime Ringlets

by Susannah Marriott
photographs David Woolford

1989 is Olave Baden-Powell's centenary. Lots of old beauty techniques work as well now as they did when Olave was young.

Take rag curling: it's perfect for producing a cascade of curls for special occasions or just gentle waves, and as good as the heated rollers available today.

In 1895 the *Girl's Own Paper* advised that, "The hair should be waved in deep curves, and this can be managed by wetting it when putting in pins for the night."

So why not curl up too? It's easy to do – even if it can make your arms ache a bit – it's gentle on your hair, and best of all it's cheap!

What you need:

J Cloths make excellent rags. Cut them into long strips, with the grain or they'll tear.

Bendy rollers (sold by numerous hair care companies) also work very well and are easy to use, although they are more expensive.

Setting lotion, gel or mousse. Although the latter are more widely available, setting lotion (your mums will remember it) still produces the best results. We put ours in a plant mist sprayer for even application.

Plenty of patience, and a friend to help you. It can be a chore curling the sections at the back of your head, so why not spend an evening in with a friend and take it in turns to wind each other's hair?

Slightly damp hair – start with it about 70/80% wet; not so damp that it drips, but not bone dry.

Unlayered shoulder-length hair or longer works best. But if your hair is shorter or layered you can still get stunning results from rag curling.

Winding – try to get the tension even throughout your hair. Beware of any irregularities, which can result in ugly kinks or straight bits! Don't forget to allow for a parting or fringe.

Experiment – a head of curls looks good with a very straight short fringe; or why not try adding just a few curls to your hair? Scattered throughout they create an interesting texture.

Remember – the smaller section of hair you use, the tighter the curl will be. Fine hair needs smaller sections. If you're lucky enough to have thick or naturally curly hair, you'll be able to produce good curls from larger rollers which needn't be left in so long. 30 minutes is really the minimum amount of time to allow for the curls to form. But if you can bear to sleep on the lumps, leaving the rags in overnight produces the best results.

For a tighter ringlet curl

· 1 ·

Divide your hair into sections, about 1–2 cm each.
It's best to use end-papers on the end of your curl –
use tissues cut into squares large enough to
cover the ends.

· 2 ·

Spray the first section if using setting lotion.

· 3 ·

Wrap the end of the section of hair in the end-paper.
Wind your hair up around the rag, leaving a piece of
cloth sticking out of the end. Twist up your hair as
you go. When you reach your scalp tie the two
ends of the cloth together.

· 4 ·

Keep winding until you cover your whole head, or
just do sections of your hair if you want a more
textured look. If you want a smooth curl, wind them
all in the same direction. For an uneven curl with
more movement, vary them.

· 5 ·

Leave for at least 30 minutes and unwind.

Joanne Piper (10) of the 2nd Morden
Company. Her thick one-length hair
was perfect for this ringlet curl.

For a long corkscrew curl

· 1 ·

Divide your hair into sections and spray.

· 2 ·

Tie the rag to the section of hair where it joins the scalp, leaving the cloth as long as possible.

· 3 ·

Wind the hair round and round the rag in a corkscrew effect. When you reach the end of this section of hair, wrap the cloth up around the coil of hair and tie it at the top. Leave and uncoil.

These curls will last until you wash your hair again, but don't brush them too hard, or your hair will go frizzy! It's best to 'dig' at it with a wide-toothed comb.

To complete your turn-of-the-century look, why not search for antique clothes? You can pick them up, often for only a few pence, at jumble sales and charity shops, while giving to a good cause as well.

Old underwear, camisole tops and bloomers especially, makes stylish wear for parties, picnics or holidays. Old nightdresses look good worn with big chunky belts, and flouncy petticoats add extra frills under short bubble skirts.

Other things to look out for include:

Lace collars and handkerchiefs
Diamante or jet brooches and earrings
Hatpins and powder compacts.

So brush up the jumble sale technique – sharpen your elbows and get in quickly – for your completely new, old-fashioned image!

◄ *Don't brush your hair for tight snake-like curls. Joanne wears a broderie-anglaise edged camisole.*

Jane Jarvis (10) of the 1st Merton Park Company with curls down to her waist. It took over two hours to get all the curlers in!
▼

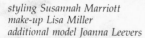

styling Susannah Marriott
make-up Lisa Miller
additional model Joanna Leevers

Take two

by Julia Nellthorp
illustration Chris Duggan

1. Which Paul Newman and Robert Redford film included the song *Raindrops Keep Falling On My Head*?
  a *The Sting*
  b *Butch Cassidy and the Sundance Kid*
  c *The Colour of Money*

2. Humphrey Bogart and Lauren Bacall eventually married each other but in which film did they first star opposite each other?
  a *The Big Sleep*
  b *To Have and Have Not*
  c *Dark Passage*

3. Clint Eastwood slipped out of his Dirty Harry role in 1978 to act opposite a rather unusual co-star called Clyde in *Every Which Way But Loose*. Was Clyde
  a an orang-utan?
  b a dog?
  c a parrot?

4. Fred Astaire and Ginger Rogers sang and danced together in nine films. In which of the following did they not work together?
  a *Flying Down to Rio*
  b *Swing Time*
  c *Daddy Longlegs*

5. Marlene Dietrich starred alongside Warner Oland in the 1932 film *Shanghai Express*. Which husband and wife team were the stars in the 1986 remake?
  a Paul Newman and Joanne Woodward
  b Madonna and Sean Penn
  c John and Bo Derek

6. From what can Pee-Wee Herman not be separated in *Pee-Wee's Big Adventure*?
  a his giant toothbrush
  b his dog Speck
  c his bicycle

7. Albert 'Cubby' Broccoli produced *Chitty Chitty Bang Bang*, but is best-known for his long-term association with a popular fictional character. Is this character
  a James Bond?
  b Lassie?
  c Rocky?

8. Which of the following comic duos are famous for the line 'That's another fine mess you've gotten us into . . .'
  a Chesney Allen and Bud Flanagan
  b Stan Laurel and Oliver Hardy
  c Dan Ackroyd and Chevy Chase.

Answers page 63.

37

STYLISH STENCILLING

by Brenda Apsley illustrations Nicola Heindl

Are you bored with your room? Fed up with plain white walls? Miserable that it has no special 'look', no co-ordination? If the answer is yes, stencilling is for you. It's the quickest, easiest, cheapest and prettiest way to transform a room, making it very much 'yours'. Here's how:

The design motif:

Choose a very simple, smooth design motif. Flower, tree and fruit outlines are ideal, as are geometric shapes, letters and numbers. Avoid fiddly outlines, such as flower stems. If you can't decide on a design, why not use the simple dove outline on this page?

The stencil:

You can buy ready-cut stencils from art and decorating shops, but it's much cheaper and quite easy to make your own. You need some special oiled stencil card (from art shops) and a craft knife. Trace your design outline onto thin paper, then lay a sheet of carbon paper between it and the stencil card. Trace firmly around the outline to transfer it to the stencil card. Now cut away the inner card shape using a craft knife. These are very sharp, so be extra careful, or ask an adult to help. The inner card edge should be smooth and curved.

Equipment:

Emulsion paint is ideal for stencilling. Use leftovers, or buy the cheap mini trial pots. Don't use gloss paint. To apply the paint you'll need a special, stubby stencilling brush, from decorating or art shops. Don't try to use an ordinary paintbrush – it won't work!

Surfaces:

You can stencil on almost any flat surface. Plain white emulsion-painted walls are ideal. Providing your motif is simple, you can also stencil on woodchip wallpaper. You can stencil on painted wooden furniture, skirting boards and doors, but make sure surfaces are smooth and grease-free.

Where to stencil:

Before you begin you must decide on the design motif, the area you will cover and the colour or colours you will use. A motif like the dove looks good in a row around all four walls at eye level, or flying in a flock on one wall. Or reverse the stencil to give a pair of doves, beak to beak, and space them evenly around the walls. Very simple repeat designs of geometric shapes or flowers look good along the top of skirting boards – you can even continue the design across furniture and doors in an unbroken line. If wall space is limited, how about a stunning multicoloured group of flower heads in a simple basket? Use quite strong colours, rather than very pale pastels, and be bold with geometric patterns – perhaps black, grey and bright red on white walls. If you want something super-simple, stencil lots of dots in different colours and sizes in groups. Look in magazines for other ideas.

Before you begin:

Plan your design on paper and keep it handy to refer to as you work. Make sure you have permission to stencil your room, and cover carpets (and yourself)!

Check that you have your materials:

stencil	foil tray for paint
stencil brush	kitchen roll
paint	masking tape

How to stencil:

1

Position the stencil and hold in place with strips of masking tape (from DIY shops).

2

Pour a little paint into a foil tray and fill your stencil brush. Don't overload the brush. Dab off some of the paint on kitchen roll – the brush should be almost dry.

3

Apply the paint, working from the outside edges in. Hold the stencil brush upright, and apply in dabs. Make sure excess paint doesn't run under the stencil.

4

Lift off the stencil CAREFULLY. Wipe off any runs with kitchen roll and leave to dry.

5

Clean the stencil, dry, and reposition for the next motif.

6

If you are using more than one colour, allow the first to dry completely before applying the second.

Use the same method for furniture, but when the design is finished and completely dry, add a layer of clear polyurethane varnish to protect it.

If you want to try more intricate stencilling, Stencil Decor make a range of ready-cut stencils and special paint crayons. They are sold in decorating shops, are very easy to apply, and look very professional.

Stencilling on fabric

To give your room a really co-ordinated look, stencil on fabric too: pillowcases, cushion covers, duvet covers, roller blinds, tablecloths, even curtains. The stencilling technique is basically the same, but you must choose washable fabrics (polycotton is ideal) and special fabric paints.

Fabric paints

Dylon produce Color Fun fabric paints in pots and pens. The pens are good for simple outlines, the paints better for larger, stencilled areas. There are 12 pot and 8 pen colours, and you can mix them with white for pastels.

Pentel make packs of small Fabricfun dye sticks that you can use in the same way.

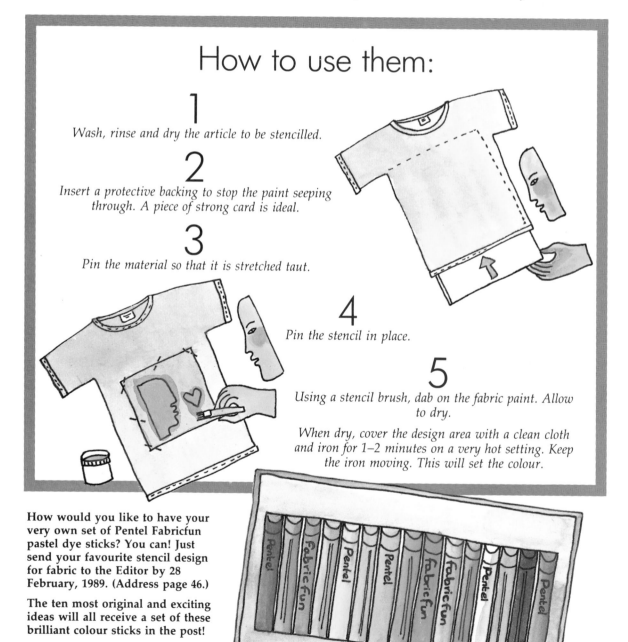

How to use them:

1
Wash, rinse and dry the article to be stencilled.

2
Insert a protective backing to stop the paint seeping through. A piece of strong card is ideal.

3
Pin the material so that it is stretched taut.

4
Pin the stencil in place.

5
Using a stencil brush, dab on the fabric paint. Allow to dry.

When dry, cover the design area with a clean cloth and iron for 1–2 minutes on a very hot setting. Keep the iron moving. This will set the colour.

How would you like to have your very own set of Pentel Fabricfun pastel dye sticks? You can! Just send your favourite stencil design for fabric to the Editor by 28 February, 1989. (Address page 46.)

The ten most original and exciting ideas will all receive a set of these brilliant colour sticks in the post!

40

FAMOUS GUIDES

by Ben Hall

Kim Wilde: from Patrol Leader to chart-topper! MCA

We read about them every day, women who have made their mark on the world in one way or another, but have you ever stopped to wonder just how many of them were Guides? You might be surprised by the answer.

Some ex-Guides have had fame thrust upon them, take The Princess Royal. Her Royal Highness has been famous from the day she was born, but never let that stand in the way of her Guiding, nor of her other love, horses. In 1971, Princess Anne achieved success in the Burghley Horse Trials in Lincolnshire, where she won the Raleigh European Three Day Event Championships. Since then, she has made a name for herself as the 'caring Princess' through her work with various charities, most notably, the Save The Children Fund. It was for this work that she was awarded the title of Princess Royal in the Birthday Honours list of 1987. The title of Princess Royal is very rarely bestowed and it has to be earned by the recipient.

Another Guide who went on to be famous for her outdoor pursuits, for quite different reasons, is Anneka Rice. You will already have seen her breathless antics in Channel 4's *Treasure Hunt* on page 10. In our exclusive interview she told us:

'Guiding was marvellous. We had a very ambitious Company. Once we went on summer camp to the Alps. It was heaven. All the mountain flowers were out; it was gorgeous. One aspect of Guiding that sticks in my mind, or should that be my nostrils, is the smell of burnt sausages over the camp fire. I'm a great fan of team spirit. I love the camaraderie on *Treasure Hunt*. We are a team working together with one aim. It's the same with Guiding, whether you are planning a project, organising a camp or doing something for charity. It's having a sense of purpose. And, of course, Guiding is great fun.'

British athlete, Fatima Whitbread, also enjoyed outdoor activities as a Guide, but says that it was the discipline that she learnt through Guiding which helped her achieve so much. Fatima is one of the all-time great female athletes, winning a gold medal at the World Athletics Championships in Rome in 1987. She has progressed further in the field sport of javelin than any other British woman, and will go down in the archives for breaking the Eastern Bloc's hold over the event.

Of the many Guides who have become famous, quite a number seem to end up on television. Popular television presenter, Sarah Greene, was a Guide. During her *Blue Peter* days Sarah had to complete almost as large a variety of challenges as Guides do, from parachute jumping to riding the *Blue Peter* pony Rags through the streets of London, in the Lord Mayor's show. Sarah, who studied at Hull University, is a talented actress as well as presenter.

The BBC seems to employ an abundance of ex-Guides. Sue Cook, who was one of the presenters on *Nationwide* and moved on to *Crimewatch UK*, is a good example. She still takes a lead in fund-raising through the Children in Need appeal, which is run every year by the BBC.

Perhaps one of the most internationally famous ex-Guides is Kim Smith. Kim who? Well, she's probably better known as Kim Wilde, international singing star and daughter of 60's pop star, Marty Wilde. Kim had a long Guiding career and even made it to Patrol Leader. These days she's better known for leading the pop charts than a Patrol, and her hits include *Kids in America*, *Chequered Love* and her massive hit from the summer of '86 *You Keep Me Hanging On*. Kim says that she loved Guiding and was involved in every activity available.

So, you see, singing in the chorus of the Gang Show or running in the egg & spoon race on Fun Day could yet be the start of something big!

Anneka Rice smiles at the memory of burnt sausages up the Alps. Michael Edwards

Princess Anne, Robin Patrol Leader, outside her tent on camp, 1963. At this point she had the Swimmer, Horsewoman and Child Nurse badges.

THE WIDGET COMPANY

by John Deft

Do you think that you could be a successful business woman, running a large company and making major policy decisions? If you have a computer at home (or if your teacher will let you use one at school) then here is a chance for you to find out just how good you might be. The computer game below puts you in charge of a company manufacturing widgets (very useful things!) and asks you to make various decisions from month to month. The game ends when you either become a millionaire or go bankrupt!

The program as listed will work on most common microcomputers, but some small changes may be needed for your particular machine. These changes are listed in the Conversion Notes below, and it is a good idea to read them before you start typing in the program. When you do start typing, be very careful to get the punctuation right and not to confuse (for example) letter O and figure 0. Once you have finished you can save the program on tape or disk so that you will not need to retype it when you want to play again.

Conversion Notes

LET can be omitted wherever it occurs, if you wish, on any common computer except the *Spectrum*.

RND(1) in lines 100, 110, 120, 250, 290, 470, 540, 670 and 680 generates a random decimal between 0 and 1. On a *Spectrum* you should change this to RND, and on a *TRS-80* to RND(0).

CLS in line 140 is an instruction to clear the screen. Replace this by HOME if you are using an *Apple* computer, or by PRINT CHR$(147) on a *Vic* or *Pet*.

If your screen width is less than 48 characters, you may need to put some extra spaces into some of the PRINTing lines, so that words are not broken in the middle – you can work out these changes yourself if need be.

Why should boys have all the fun with computers? This is your chance to try *your* game, even if you have to use your elbows to get a turn at the keyboard! Type it in, save it, then RUN the game and see how you get on. Ready . . . steady . . .

```
100 LET X=1u0*INT(RND(1)*100)
110 LET M=1 : LET M1=INT(RND(1)*12)
120 LET F=10*INT(RND(1)*20+30)
130 LET C1=5000 : LET P4=5000
140 CLS
150 PRINT "MONTHLY SITUATION REPORT – MONTH";M
160 PRINT "CASH IN HAND";X;"POUNDS"
170 PRINT "IN STOCK";W;"WIDGETS AND";T;"TREES"
180 IF X>=0 THEN LET X1=0 : LET X2=0 : GOTO 230
190 LET X2=X2+1 : IF X2<3 THEN 230
200 PRINT "THE BANK INSIST YOU REDUCE YOUR OVERDRAFT!"
210 IF X>X1 OR X2<6 THEN LET X1=X : GOTO 230
220 PRINT "IN FACT, YOU ARE BANKRUPT!!" : GOTO 780
230 PRINT
240 IF X>1000000 THEN PRINT "YOU ARE A MILLIONAIRE!" : GOTO 780
250 LET P=1000*INT(1+RND(1)*P4/500)
260 PRINT "YOU HAVE PROVISIONAL ORDERS FOR";P;"WIDGETS"
270 PRINT
280 PRINT "EACH WIDGET TREE WILL MAKE 100 WIDGETS"
290 LET S=20*INT(RND(1)*5+5)
300 PRINT "WIDGET TREES COST";S;"POUNDS EACH"
310 PRINT "HOW MANY WIDGET TREES WILL YOU ORDER";
320 INPUT T1
330 LET T=T+T1 : LET Z1=T*100
340 PRINT
350 PRINT "EACH WORKER CAN MAKE 200 WIDGETS PER MONTH"
360 PRINT "AT PRESENT YOU EMPLOY";E;"WORKERS"
370 PRINT "HOW MANY EXTRA WORKERS WILL YOU HIRE";
380 INPUT E1
390 PRINT "HOW MANY WORKERS WILL YOU DISMISS";
400 INPUT E2
410 IF E2>E+E1 THEN 360
420 LET E=E+E1-E2 : LET Z2=E*200
430 LET C4=E*100 : IF C1<C4 THEN LET C1=C4
440 PRINT
450 PRINT "AT PRESENT EACH WORKER EARNS";F;"POUNDS A MONTH"
460 IF M1<12 THEN 620
470 LET F1=10*INT(RND(1)*9+2)
480 PRINT "THEY ARE ASKING FOR A WAGE RISE OF";F1;"POUNDS"
490 PRINT "WILL YOU PAY WHAT THEY ASK (Y/N)";
500 INPUT Z$
510 IF Z$="Y" THEN 590
520 PRINT "WHAT RISE WILL YOU OFFER";
530 INPUT F2
540 LET R=RND(1) : IF F2>R*F1 THEN 580
550 PRINT "ALL YOUR WORKERS HAVE GONE ON STRIKE"
560 PRINT "YOU CANNOT MAKE ANY WIDGETS THIS MONTH"
570 LET Z2=0 : LET C2=T1*S : LET C3=0 : GOTO 630
580 LET F1=F2
590 LET F=F+F1
600 PRINT "EACH WORKER NOW EARNS";F;"POUNDS A MONTH"
610 LET M1=0
620 LET C2=T1*S : LET C3=(E+2*E2)*F
630 PRINT
640 PRINT "HOW MUCH WILL YOU CHARGE FOR EACH WIDGET SOLD";
650 INPUT V
660 LET V1=S/100+F/200+C1/P
670 LET P1=1000*INT(RND(1)*20)
680 LET P2=1000*INT(RND(1)*20*(V-V1)) : IF V<V1 THEN LET P2=0
690 LET P3=P+P1-P2 : IF P3<0 THEN LET P3=0
700 IF Z1>Z2 THEN LET Z=Z2
710 IF Z1<=Z2 THEN LET Z=Z1
720 LET W=W+Z : LET T=T-Z/100 : IF P3>W THEN LET P3=W
730 PRINT "YOU SOLD";P3;"WIDGETS THIS MONTH"
740 IF P4<P3 THEN LET P4=P3
750 FOR I=1 TO 500 : NEXT I
760 LET W=W-P3 : LET X=X-C1-C2-C3+P3*V : LET M=M+1 : LET M1=M1+1
770 GOTO 140
780 PRINT : PRINT : END
```

BY VIV QUILLIN

Syncopated
SYMPHONY

'When you say the Scout and Guide Orchestra, everyone always says "Huh, a load of squares". But we're not, it's well smart,' says Tracy, a trumpet player.

The National Scout and Guide Symphony Orchestra are on their week-long residential course at Orwell Park School near Ipswich. I visited them and what I saw convinced me Tracy was right.

Two of the Orchestra's most eligible young men: Nick, violin, and Neil, leader of the cellos.

Fiona (left) from Nottinghamshire with her horn, and Tracy with her trumpet.

From left to right: Tracy, Sophia and Angela pose with paddles.

by Susannah Marriott
photographs David Woolford

What musical standard are you?

'Brilliant.' Not too prone to modesty is our Nick, a Lancashire Venture Scout. In fact most of the members of the Orchestra are over Grade 8. They first sight-read the music they're to play on arrival, Friday evening. By Wednesday of the next week they have to perform in public. That takes an enormous amount of work, and great skill.

Musical likes:

'Dire Straits, Meatloaf, U2 and whatever's on the jukebox.'

Event of the week:

'This interview. And my sleeping bag went out of the window last night.'

Tracy's an old hand – she's been with the Orchestra for three years now and says, 'Everyone makes you really welcome.'

What's it like working with Scouts?

'They're a laugh. We were joking last night that there's not enough to go round – there's only about ten fellas!'

That's in an Orchestra of over 60 members from all over the UK, including Ulster and Scotland.

Event of the week:

'Swimming in the outdoor pool at midnight last night! It was floodlit from beneath and about thirty of us played water polo for an hour. It was really warm in there even though it was so cold outside.'

As well as an exhausting six hours rehearsal a day, there's plenty of leisure time; for watching videos, kite-flying or canoeing (very popular). The school's grounds include a swimming pool, tennis and squash courts and even a golf course.

Musical likes:

'*Mars* and *Jupiter* by Holst. It's great to play in this Orchestra as it's pretty good musically.'

Sophia, violin, should know, it's her sixth year. But Sophie and Angela, bassoon, have pretty weird likes beyond the classics. They listen to indie bands like Primal Scream, The Shop Assistants and Half Man Half Biscuit. Very unusual for a Brown Owl – that's what Sophie is working towards.

What are the tutors like?

'They're really nice – good fun to work with.'

All the tutors are associated with leading London orchestras and really enjoy working with such talented musicians.

Joanne, a 13-year-old flute player and Guide from Grimsby told me, 'Sometimes they get a bit mad if you can't get it right, but they're all right really.' The different sections proved this, giving their tutors thank you presents while I was there.

Christopher, this angelic-looking 14-year-old Scout from Wakefield, isn't just a brilliant cellist, he's also the most mischievous lad in the Orchestra.

Some of the string section in the grounds of Orwell Park School.

Sally, second from right, is a violinist from Belgium (British Scouts in Western Europe). 'I belong to the largest County, from Norway to Cyprus,' she boasts.

What's it like touring abroad?

'That's the best bit. Last year we toured in Germany and Vienna. The journey's good. We get to sit in the coach and spend two days bowing all the first and second violin parts! Everybody sits round and goes "Up, Down, Up, Down".'

Everyone was looking forward to touring Japan in 1988.

Most exciting event:

'Last year in Bonn on the Vienna Tour was fun. It was the last night abroad, so I dressed up as a punk – Sophie did me up just like her – all the make-up, the lot. Then we went out and got some very odd reactions!

'I'm usually the one that gets put in anything – all the messes. I've been in a double bass case before. I got out of a xylophone case in the middle of rehearsal once and shocked George the conductor!'

What's the food like?

Claire, a 14-year-old first-time violinist said, 'The food's all right, but the cold baked beans at every meal get to you after a bit! And the salad. It's not bad salad, it's just constant salad!'

Sally adds, 'It's not as bad as Germany though. All we ate there was salami and dry bread – every single day!'

Matthew, percussion, and Mia, violin – the togetherness of Guiding and Scouting!

I watched the Orchestra in full rehearsal with George and he certainly put them through their paces. It all sounded faultless to my untutored ear, but he kept interrupting, hitting his baton on the lectern – 'Come on, you're going to do it till you've got it right.'

And they did get it right. That's one thing *everyone* was determined to do!

Japan here they come!

If you're a musician and would like to join the National Scout and Guide Symphony Orchestra, why not ask your Guider for more information or write to the Programme Department, CHQ?

WIN A SYNTHESIZER

You may not be as musically accomplished as the members of the Scout and Guide Orchestra, but anyone who has access to a tape recorder can enter this year's competition.

photograph Casio

Casio has donated a brand new SK1 sampling keyboard, as raved about in the music press. As well as providing a full range of keyboard sounds and rhythm box, this synthesizer allows you to record snippets of sounds — car engines, dogs barking, the radio, even yourself! — and mix them in while you play. You too can be a hip hop rapping DJ with this keyboard! What do you have to do to win this excellent prize? Simply send us a tape recording of a song or piece of music you've written, either on your own, with your Patrol, or with a group of friends. It can be in any musical style and on any subject, but it must be an original song, not more than four minutes long.

The winner will receive the SK1 Keyboard in the post.

Don't forget to include your name, address, age and Guide Company with your entry, and please tell us what you'd like to see in next year's Annual.

Happy music-making!

Send your entries by March 31, 1989 to:

The Editor
The Girl Guide Annual
The Girl Guides Association
17–19 Buckingham Palace Road
London
SW1W 0PT

46

Twenty clues are given here. Each one represents a number. Can you supply the number for each clue? Check your answers on page 63.

A A baker's dozen.
B The number you score when you score a score.
C Throw the 'r' away from this bridge to Wales.
D The Prime Minister's lodgings in Downing Street.
E How many Sisters on the Kent coast plus ten?
F The quantity of a pair.
G Half the blackbirds baked in a pie.
H One year less than two decades.
I Half a dozen.
J How many Ladies in this Derbyshire stone circle?

K The days in a fortnight.
L The age of majority.
M Petits whats are sweets?
N The number of Oaks in this Kentish town?
O One less than a dozen.
P Three sets of quintuplets.
Q The minutes in a twelfth of an hour.
R The Firth of what is the estuary of a river running between Fife and Lothian?
S How many people in two eightsome reel sets?
T A pair of quads.

TWENTY-TWENTY Quiz

WHAT'S THE COLOUR

Red, yellow and blue are primary colours.
If you mix them together, you get the secondary
colours orange, green and violet. White isn't a colour and black is a mix of all the colours.
Here is a colour chart showing all these colours. Each colour contains a clue. Your answer
will be a word with that colour in it. Write your answer for each colour here, and check it on
page 63.

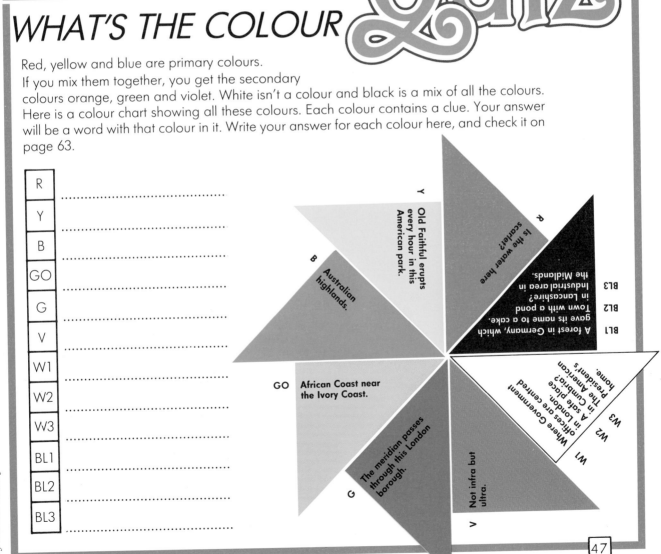

R	....
Y	....
B	....
GO	....
G	....
V	....
W1	....
W2	....
W3	....
BL1	....
BL2	....
BL3	....

Y Old Faithful erupts every hour in this American park.

R Is the water here scarlet?

BL3 Industrial area in the Midlands.

BL2 Town with a pond in Lancashire?

BL1 A forest in Germany, which gave its name to a cake.

B Australian highlands.

GO African Coast near the Ivory Coast.

G The meridian passes through this London borough.

V Not infra but ultra.

W1 Where Government offices are centred in London.

W2 A safe place in Cumbria?

W3 The American President's home.

by Deborah Manley

ON YOUR BMX

by Tony Rose
photographs Tony Rose

The riders jam their front wheels against a vertical board. On the countdown of "Riders ready, pedals ready, Go!" it drops flat and they're off. Legs going like pistons, they jerk from side to side through a spectacular series of berms, holes and jumps before a mad dash for the finish line – that's if they're skilled enough to be still on the bike!

Do you remember your first bike ride? Well BMX cycle racing is about as far removed from that tentative moment as the final stages of the Milk Race. However they do have one thing in common – there's a great deal of falling off involved! At any BMX race meeting you'll find over one hundred girls competing, in age groups ranging from 6 and under through to 16. Many are turned out in brightly-coloured garb like American footballers.

I attended a meeting of over 500 races, with competitors from all over Britain and abroad. Claire Edwards (13) and Lisa Wright (15) ride for sponsors GT Factory, and are champions in their age groups. Claire viewed the day's racing with some trepidation, as the starting gate was slipping early on. Lisa, the UK number one, had suffered a patchy season up-to-date. Although she'd won her first national meeting, a couple of spills in the last two races had put her under some pressure. She summed up what made a good BMX rider in two words, "having guts". Tactics are a bit limited – "getting out of the start gate first and going like mad."

Luli Abeyemo (15) is a cheerful ex-Guide from Newark near Nottingham. This was her first day of Profile-sponsored racing and her fate would be decided in race 91. Luli started like all the girls, racing locally with her own bike. Her boyfriend took her to some national meets which, as she puts it rather shyly, "I just kept winning, so I got picked out!" I found out later that Luli was in fact world champion in her age group. When she races locally her friends turn out to support her. Asked whether they had shown any interest in taking part she laughed, "No. They're a bit scared."

After a bad start, ex-Guide Luli Abeyemo moves up on the leader. Asked what makes a good rider she says "Courage, strength and determination."
▼

Champions all. Left to right: Claire Edwards, Luli Abeyemo and Lisa Wright.
▼

BMX racing is a tough, physically demanding and highly competitive sport, but on-track rivalry aside, many friendships are made as the girls keep meeting up throughout the season.

◄ After the Bomb Hole (in which several riders come to grief), two spectacular jumps called The Camels. Some of the riders find time to incorporate a trick or two, twisting the front wheel at right angles in mid-air, then straightening up before landing. The wisest riders try not to jump the next set of bumps. Leaving terra firma looks good, but if you land on your front forks, instead of winning you end up in an embarrassing heap!

◀ Claire Edwards leans into the berm (corner). At this point she's way out in front and went on to win not only this moto (heat) but also her final. Each race takes about 35 seconds at the most, but this doesn't include time for clearing bikes and bodies off the track!

How do you get started in the sport?
The bike is naturally the most expensive item – prices range from £99 to £1000. An alternative might be to do up a second-hand bike. A helmet will cost anything from £10 to £100, but they can be hired out for as little as £2 a day. All you need otherwise is a pair of gloves, a long-sleeved sweatshirt and some old jeans.

Unfortunately there's no way round the initial outlay, but if you are a successful rider and get spotted by one of the large bike manufacturers, such as Raleigh, GT Factory or Profile, you could be offered sponsorship. This not only means a free bike and helmet, but also a one-piece suit in the sponsor's racing colours and logo.

To find out about BMX clubs in your area, or for more information, contact UK BMX Association, London House, 42 Upper Richmond Road West, London SW14 8DD.

And what of Luli, Claire and Lisa? All got through to their finals and won! We wish them luck in their future BMX careers.

▲ Sweeping down from the start the riders jostle for position. BMX racing draws large crowds and with a commentator on a tannoy system and the cheers and whistles, it takes little imagination to transport the scene to Brands Hatch!

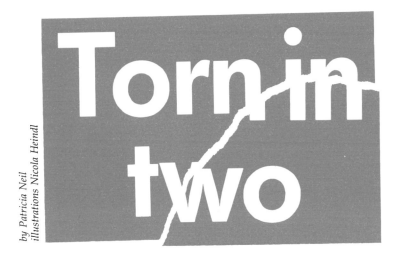

Torn in two

by Patricia Neil
illustrations Nicola Heindl

There was something different about Lesley at the moment. Gill, Susie and Nicola had noticed – well, they would, as they saw each other every day. But even Gary Nesbit of 5W had turned round towards her in his seat on the school bus on Monday evening and said, 'What's shut you up today, then?' The thought that Gary Nesbit had actually noticed one of them, and noticed enough to make a comment, was pretty amazing – but it didn't seem to affect Lesley.

By Wednesday lunch-time, things were getting serious. 'You're going to have to tell us what's wrong, you know, Lesley,' said Gill.

'Look,' said Lesley, taking an age to unwrap her sandwiches, so she didn't have to look at Gill while she spoke, 'I *have* got something on my mind . . . and I suppose you think I've been a bit off this week.'

'Yes, you have!' said Susie, 'I specially kept a place for you in the art room and you went and sat in that corner seat on your own instead.'

Nicola reckoned that now would be a good moment to express her resentment too. 'You promised to bring your new tape in so I could borrow it – but when I reminded you, you just snapped at me . . .'

Gill looked at Lesley and saw how shamefaced she was. 'It doesn't matter; we're all still friends,' she reassured her quickly. 'But we might be able to help – if you let us.'

Lesley shook her head. 'You can't,' she said quietly. 'It's something I have to sort out myself. Can we drop it?' And she glanced up at the other three pleadingly.

'Okay,' said Gill. 'But remember – you can tell us anything and we'll keep it a secret if you want us to.'

'I know. Thanks.'

That evening, Lesley got off the school bus before her usual stop. This gave her the chance to be on her own for a short while, and if she walked the long way down Etherstone Crescent instead of cutting through the alleyway, she was likely to avoid seeing anyone from school hanging about.

For the tenth time that day, Lesley wondered what on earth she was going to do. And she wished for the hundredth time she could turn the clock back to last Friday – before she faced her problem. Then she thought again. 'If I'm honest, I'd turn the clock back five years.'

It wasn't that life had been uncomplicated then though, she had to admit. Mum and Dad used to have dreadful rows and she remembered a time – she must have been about six – when they didn't speak to one another for a whole week. It was awful. The atmosphere would be cold and so unwelcoming when she came in from school. Sometimes, things would be a bit better for a time. Mum and Dad would try not to argue in front of her – but she'd know when they were angry with each other again, even if they weren't shouting.

At night Lesley would lie awake, not wanting to listen, but unable not to. The voices would start and there'd be another argument, ending with the sound of Mum's sobs, the slam of the front door and the noise of the car starting up. Dad would be driving off in a temper again.

One night – it was the night of her eighth birthday, Lesley remembered – Dad had come upstairs, as he often did, to switch off her light and say good night. This time, he sat on her bed and put his arms round her. 'Lesley, love,' he said at last, 'your Mum and I argue a lot, don't we?'

Lesley nodded.

'I'm sorry. Mum's sorry too. The last thing we want is to make you unhappy.'

'I know,' Lesley whispered.

'Remember,' Dad had continued, 'whatever happens to Mum and I, we'll always love you.' Then he kissed her and went downstairs. A week later, Lesley came home from school and Mum told her Dad had left – they were going to get a divorce.

Dad had kept his promise. He had carried on loving her, as Mum had too, of course. Lesley went to stay with her father most weekends. He decorated a room especially for her and she was able to keep some of her things there permanently.

Mum never objected to her going to Dad's – but she hardly ever asked about what she'd done at the weekend. In fact Lesley's two worlds hardly touched at all. Dad would pick Lesley up from school on a Friday afternoon and then bring her back home first thing on Monday morning so she could pick up her school books, dropping her off without getting out of the car himself. In the five years Mum and Dad had been apart, Lesley reckoned they could only have spoken to each other four or five times.

Yes, there was a fairly smooth routine. Yes, Lesley knew both Mum and Dad cared a lot about her. But just sometimes Lesley felt like two people – Dad's daughter Friday to Monday, and Mum's daughter Monday to Friday. She never seemed to have the chance to be just Lesley, with a mother and father in the background.

'Hey!'

The voice behind her made her jump. She turned round. It was Gill.

'Didn't you hear me yelling?' she asked Lesley. 'I saw you at the end

51

of the street when I came out of the dentist's.'

'Sorry, I was thinking. I never heard you,' said Lesley.

'All clear, thank goodness,' said Gill laughing.

'All clear?' Lesley was puzzled.

'At the dentist! No fillings – and he says I don't need to wear my wires any more!' For several months, Gill had had to wear a brace to straighten her teeth.

'Oh good!' Lesley knew how Gill had loathed her 'wires'. 'Listen, why don't you stop by my house before you go home – I can give you that tape for Nicola.' However, the real reason Lesley had made her suggestion was to make up for her distant behaviour that week. Gill was her best friend, but Lesley knew she hadn't been treating her like one.

'Great!' Gill replied. The two smiled at each other and walked on towards Lesley's house.

Lesley looked anxiously at her mother, who was lying back in the armchair, watching her daughter make a cup of tea for the three of them. 'How're you feeling, Mum?'

'Honestly, love, better every day,' Mrs Rainton answered. 'The doctors said it would take me a few weeks to recover completely from the operation, you know, so I should expect to feel tired, shouldn't I? But things aren't too busy in the shop at the moment and they let me take a break whenever I want.'

'I'm just glad to have you home again,' said Lesley, giving her mother a hug.

'Yes, and I'm glad I'm home as well,' said Mrs Rainton. 'I didn't like the thought of you staying with your dad when I was in hospital. That long bus ride back to his house after school and then having to wait in on your own until he came back from work . . .'

Lesley felt uncomfortable, as she always did on the occasions Mum talked about Dad, especially in front of Gill.

'Still, I'm okay now,' her mother went on. 'And with our holiday to look forward to, I feel as if I'm really getting back to normal.'

'Are you off on holiday, then?' asked Gill.

'Yes – didn't Lesley say? I booked it at the weekend. Dr Hodges said a fortnight's rest in a relaxing place – those were her exact words! – would be the final cure! Lesley and I are taking a beach-side apartment in Menorca next month,' said Mrs Rainton.

'Smashing!' said Gill, enviously. 'Think of all that sun compared to this rotten wet spring we're having. Bet you can't wait, Lesley!'

Lesley didn't answer immediately. 'Yes,' she said quietly after a pause. 'Look, Gill, here's your tea. Come up to my room and you can listen to the tape.'

Gill flopped down on Lesley's bed. 'Hey, you're really lucky, you know. Two weeks off school and you'll come back with a great suntan. That'll make Gary Nesbit take more notice. Why didn't you tell us about it?'

Lesley looked up from the cassette recorder. 'I don't know if I'm going yet.'

Gill was confused. 'But your mum said she'd booked . . .'

'I know. She really wants to go and to take me with her. She'd be worried about being ill, too, if there was no-one with her. But I still don't know if I can go.'

'Why? Oh . . . this is all to do with the way you've been acting this week, isn't it?' Gill asked.

'Yes, it is,' Lesley admitted.

Gill was immediately sympathetic. 'Go on. Tell me about it. I might have some brilliant ideas.'

Lesley sighed. 'I don't suppose you will – but I'll tell you anyway. Like I said earlier on though, it's something I have to sort out for myself.'

'Try me, go on,' urged Gill.

'Well, when I was at Dad's last weekend, Cassie was there. Have you ever met her?'

Gill nodded. 'Your dad's girlfriend? I thought you liked her.'

'I do,' insisted Lesley. 'She's really nice. They've been together about two years now. She's divorced as well and she's got a little boy . . .'

'Yes, I remember Charlie. He's lovely!'

'Anyway, Dad and Cassie told me they're going to get married. I was so pleased. When the four of us are together, I feel we're a real family.' Lesley lowered her eyes, ashamed. She felt guilty, thinking and talking like that – almost as if she was being disloyal to Mum.

'Go on,' said Gill. 'That was good news then, wasn't it?'

'Not really, well, rather yes and no.' Lesley hesitated. 'You see, they asked me to be bridesmaid, with Charlie as a pageboy. The date's been booked for the 22nd.'

'The time you're supposed to be in Menorca with your mum?' Gill asked.

'Right. Of course, I'd already said yes to Dad and Cassie, and when I got here on Monday morning Mum was full of the holiday. I just couldn't tell her – she'd have been so hurt to think I was putting Dad's wedding before her, I mean, our holiday.'

'I see,' said Gill, thoughtfully. 'And telling your dad you couldn't be bridesmaid would look as if you were putting your mum first?'

'That's it, exactly,' said Lesley. 'I love them both the same, and sometimes I feel as if I've got to be showing I love them the same all the time. It's hard to cope with. And I don't know what to do . . .' Her voice faltered and she reached for a tissue.

'There must be something you can do . . . they could change the wedding date, or your mum could re-book the holiday,' suggested Gill.

'Yes, I know,' said Lesley through her tears, 'but that would let one think I wanted to do one thing more than the other ... d'you see?'

Gill did see. 'I'm going to have a think about this, Lesley. Don't worry too much about it. Something will work out.'

The next day Lesley went out of school at lunch-time as usual, to buy herself a bar of chocolate. She was surprised to see Cassie at the school gates.

'Hi, Lesley,' said Cassie. 'I thought I might catch you if I waited here!'

'Cassie! It's nice to see you.' Lesley was pleased, but puzzled.

Cassie paused. 'If you're going to the shop, maybe I can come with you and buy you a Coke or something in Harrington's Cafe.'

Lesley nodded. 'Yes, great.'

They took a table in a quiet alcove. Lesley waited. Cassie seemed to want to say something.

'Lesley,' Cassie began, 'I hear you've been double-booked, or rather your dad and I have double-booked you.'

Lesley hesitated. 'Why d'you say that?'

Cassie smiled. 'You know, this town's really quite small. Your friend Gill has an older sister, Mandy who's in great demand as a babysitter, hasn't she? I have an evening class on a Wednesday, and my regular sitter Angela couldn't make it last night. She recommended Mandy. When I answered the door to her last night, I found I had two sitters for the price of one.'

'Gill, you mean?'

'Got it in one. Mandy said she was babysitting a boy called Charlie – and Gill insisted on coming.'

'She shouldn't have said anything to you,' Lesley murmured, 'it's got nothing to do with her.'

'Look, Lesley, she's your best friend, she tells me, and she was worried about you. I didn't mind her talking to me one bit.'

'Cassie,' Lesley started to say, 'I don't know what Gill's said exactly, but you have to know I think it's just great that you and Dad are getting married ...'

'I know, Lesley,' said Cassie, gently.

'... And I don't want Dad to feel I don't want to be there ... if you know what I mean.' Lesley laughed, despite herself, but she could see Cassie understood just what she was saying.

'Lesley, can I ask you to leave it to me?' Cassie asked. 'And I'll sort something out. Just trust me.'

Lesley looked up and nodded. Yes, she thought, Cassie *would* sort something out.

That evening, Lesley came home from school and stopped short as she came towards her front door. She recognised Cassie's rusty old Mini parked outside. Was Cassie actually there, in the house with Mum?

She went up to the door, opened it as quietly as she could and slipped in. She heard voices from the living room. She went straight in and there, sitting down, were Mum, Dad, Cassie and little Charlie, who was drinking squash out of Lesley's old plastic beaker.

'Hello, love,' said Dad. 'Surprised?' And he smiled.

'A bit,' said Lesley and she sat down beside Mum on the settee. She felt awkward and she could feel she wasn't the only one. Just then, Cassie stood up and taking Charlie's hand she whispered to him to put his drink down. With a quiet, 'Bye – and thanks,' to Lesley's mother she went out, still holding Charlie's hand. 'No, it's okay, I'll see myself out,' she added as Mrs Rainton got up as well.

In answer to Lesley's questioning look, Mum spoke up. 'Your Dad and I know about each other's plans now, Lesley, and it was unfair that you were made to feel so worried ...'

'We've been talking,' said Dad. 'Cassie as well. No, I won't pretend it was easy, but we managed it. And we – your mum and I – have to take some blame for the way things have made you feel.'

'And we don't just mean last week, mind,' said Mrs Rainton, 'but before as well, when you've not felt able to talk to me about Dad ...'

'... or to me about Mum,' added Mr Rainton.

'I've been on the phone to the travel agent just now,' said Mrs Rainton. 'I can change the dates of the holiday – there's no problem.'

Lesley's father came and sat on the settee as well and leant over to hug his daughter. 'And you'll be a perfect bridesmaid!' he said.

Just for a moment Lesley felt something of what might have been; the three of them smiling, sitting together in their own home, and feeling happy in each other's company ... if life had been different, of course.

'Will you bring your worries to either one of us from now on?' asked her mother. 'And trust us to get together to sort something out when we have to?'

Lesley smiled and nodded.

Dad got up to go. He hugged Lesley again. 'Have a good holiday – you too, Barbara.' And he left.

Mum looked at Lesley. 'There's something else you need to know, love.'

'What's that?' asked Lesley.

Her mother smiled. 'You'd better go upstairs and start packing. Our flight leaves at six tomorrow morning! I've already phoned the school and the shop.'

Lesley's mood changed straightaway. 'Great! I've just got to do one thing,' she smiled.

'Tell me.'

'I have to phone Gill – and just thank her for being a friend!'

BOWED OVE[R]

Ribbon is great. It's cheap, comes in all sorts of fabrics, widths, colours and patterns, and just a metre or two can transform your hair, clothes or even your shoes. You don't need to be an expert needlewoman – you just need lots of ideas. Here are some to inspire you!

Formal, flat bows are easy to make. ▶ Grosgrain, velvet or satin ribbon works well, about 35–55mm wide. Cut a piece of ribbon three times the width of the finished bow, plus 5cm. Cut the ends diagonally. Fold the ribbon in half and stitch across the middle. Cut a short piece of ribbon about 8–10cm long and wrap it around the middle of the bow, overlapping on the wrong side. Carefully stitch the wrap-around piece to the bow and you have a flat Fergie bow. Stitch to a headband, comb or slide, or wear it on hat elastic.

◀ *For a gathered bow* use stiff ribbon about 40mm wide. Cut one piece about 20cm long, another about 14cm long. Fold the ends of each piece to the middle and lay the shorter piece on top of the longer piece. Using matching cotton, stitch from top to bottom through the middle using tacking stitches. Pull the cotton to gather the bow and tie off the cotton thread.

Make ribbon rosettes using about ▶ 15cm of 20–25mm wide ribbon. Ideally, choose a soft type that won't fray. Using matching cotton thread, stitch in small tacking stitches along one side of the ribbon, close to the edge. When you reach the end, pull the cotton tight, gathering the ribbon. Ease it into a round rosette and stitch the two ends of ribbon together.

by Brenda Apsley
illustrations Frances Lloyd

Just half a metre of soft, satin ribbon about 50mm wide makes a simple hair bow. Knot once, then tie a neat bow (just as you would on a shoelace). Cut the ends into diagonals or fishtails if the ribbon starts to fray. Wear the bow around a ponytail or at the nape of the neck.

● If you want to make a trendy stubby topknot, tie your hair up with an elastic band into a high ponytail, with the ends of your hair tucked into the same band. Then wind lots of ribbon round and round and tie to secure.

● If you have long hair, tie it into a high ponytail and secure with an elastic band. Knot three lengths of fine ribbon together and slip the knot under the elastic band. Plait your ponytail, taking up one piece of ribbon with each section of hair. Ask a friend to help you get a really professional look. Secure the ends of hair with a small elastic band, and trim off any spare bits of ribbon, or tie into a bow.

● If you have short hair – and are daring – buy some very fine satin ribbon, about 3mm wide, and cut it into pieces 12–15cm long. Tie tiny bows around tiny bunches of hair, around the hairline, or all over! You can buy pre-cut fine ribbons in packs of toning or contrasting colours which are ideal for this.

● For a floppy bow on short hair, tie a neat ribbon bow, and stitch it to a fine headband or slide using matching cotton thread. Wear three bows on a headband, or one over each ear. If you prefer, stitch to fine hat elastic knotted into a band to fit your head.

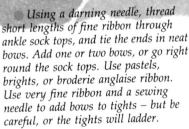

Make your trainers or DM lace-ups look different by replacing the laces with ribbon. Buy about a metre for each shoe, and thread through just like ordinary laces, knotting the ends if the ribbon is likely to fray. Use plains or patterns – or a different colour in each shoe. Buy lots of ribbon laces and co-ordinate your feet with lots of different looks.

● Clip-on bows for shoes are trendy but expensive. Copy the idea by making pairs of flat bows, gathered bows or rosettes (as opposite). You can add interesting buttons, badges or even rows of safety pins to jazz up the bows! Glue them onto the front, side, even the heels of shoes. This is permanent, so make sure you really like the bows before you stick them down. If you don't want permanent bows, cheat! Just tie lengths of soft ribbon around your feet, put on your shoes, and tuck in the bits you don't want people to see, showing just bows at the front.

● Using a darning needle, thread short lengths of fine ribbon through ankle sock tops, and tie the ends in neat bows. Add one or two bows, or go right round the sock tops. Use pastels, brights, or broderie anglaise ribbon. Use very fine ribbon and a sewing needle to add bows to tights – but be careful, or the tights will ladder.

● Hold up fashionable, over-the-knee floppy socks or stockings with soft ribbons tied in a gentle bow.

● Customise your old black woolly tights – add six or seven different colour bows up the back. Makes heads turn when worn with a boring black mini!

● Make your own garters with tags to hold up knee-length socks. To a band of elastic tight enough to hold up a sock, sew two oblongs of ribbon, cut into 'V's at the end. Black and white or navy and cream look good, or why not try tartan for an authentic Scottish look?

Your home is in trouble!

by Alan Pearson
illustrations Susannah English

If you could see the Earth from outer space, you'd see how totally isolated it is. This means that we have limited supplies of everything, and we can't get more from outside. It also means we have to live with whatever mess we make.

Many things we use like air and water are recyclable or re-usable, so there is no danger of them running out. On the other hand, many resources, like metals, coal and oil, are limited: it takes millions of years to make any more, so there is a very real danger of using them all up. Although these products may not be as vital to us as air and water, they are still very important: they make electricity, light and heat our homes, provide fuel for cars, trains and aeroplanes, and make thousands of everyday things (even plastic is made from oil).

There is another danger. As the number of people in the world and their demand for things increases, we are running out of land, and spoiling what little there is left. Forests are cut down for farmland or poisoned by acid rain. The sea, rivers and lakes become polluted, and the plants and animals in them die. The result is deserts on every inhabited continent. Another species of animal becomes extinct every day at least, possibly as fast as one an hour.

Something must be done very quickly, and it is up to everyone to help. You can start in your own home, your school, and in the environment around you. If everyone makes their own contribution, however small, we can make a difference on a world-wide scale.

Let's start with the problem of using up our resources. Many things we use every day are made from materials which are in limited supply. Help by re-using these things, or recycling the materials they are made from wherever possible.

Plastic bags and containers

can be saved and re-used, so less need to be made, less oil wasted and less pollution produced. If you can use free carriers from supermarkets as bin liners, for example, you've already used one piece of plastic twice. Try to buy brands of food which are packed in cardboard and paper containers, rather than plastic, because these are made from wood, and more trees can be grown. The plastic ones, when burnt, may also send out harmful gases into the atmosphere. Above all, don't buy over-packaged products.

56

Paper

don't waste it. The more paper we use, the more trees must be cut down. When you go shopping try to refuse paper bags in the market or at the chemist. Put everything in one carrier bag. Re-use old envelopes – buy Oxfam's re-usable labels or make your own. Save suitable scrap paper for telephone messages and shopping lists, and your old newspapers for recycling.

Your Guide Company may already collect and sell newspapers back to a local paper mill as a means of raising funds. If not, why not start, or collect them for a local charity which is already doing it? Try and find out what else can be collected for recycling. Does your town have a bottle bank? Does anyone in your area collect aluminium foil or ring-pulls?

Compost heaps

lots of families have one. If you grow flowers, fruit or vegetables then the substances that the plants take from the ground need to be replaced. You can help their

recycling by making compost from waste food, dead leaves and cuttings etc., then adding it to the soil. Gardening books will give you all the details.

Chemicals

perhaps you use them thoughtlessly around the home. Detergents and pesticides for killing insects can build up in concentration in the environment, and harm other animals. The gases used in aerosol cans are destroying the Earth's atmosphere. This might sound far-fetched but remember that the atmosphere is very thin like the skin on an apple, and that we release about a million tonnes of these gases (called chlorofluorocarbons or CFCs) every year. It would seem sensible then to use less aerosols. Which products in your house really need

to come from an aerosol? Do you really need those products anyway? Try using polish in tins, deodorant in roll-on form and hair gel in tubs, instead of mousse.

Litter

don't drop it, it's the simplest way to poison our planet! Litter spoils any view, can be unhygienic and even dangerous, especially to animals.

How about the plants and animals that are threatened? Nature can usually miraculously repair itself given the chance and enough time, but we still need to help.

In this country (and in most other places around the world) plants and animals are dying because the different places where they live, habitats, have been changed or destroyed. For example, frogs and dragonflies are much less common than they once were, partly because there are fewer ponds and ditches about. Wildflowers are now less common too, as they were often regarded as weeds, and removed or

killed. The butterflies that feed on them, either as caterpillars or adults, therefore also get more scarce, especially with the additional threat of pesticides put out for other insects.

Most of the natural habitats in this country, e.g. woodland, grassland, moorlands and marshes, are being reduced or altered, making them unsuitable for their natural inhabitants. In their place we are extending cities, roads and farmland, which don't hold the same variety of life.

In practical terms you can help a lot here. Start by encouraging wildlife around your home.

Bird tables

you may already have one in your garden to help birds in harsh weather. If not, buy one from the RSPB, a local garden centre or make your own. Many books show you how to make them, and they needn't be complicated. If you don't have a garden, buy feeding trays that can be attached to your window, or just hang up a peanut basket. Most pet shops sell wild bird seed mixtures and peanut baskets, with suitable peanuts to go in them: don't use the salted or dry-roast type! I usually recommend a wire or plastic basket, rather than the thin net bags which are sold, as they are stronger and more likely to survive over-enthusiastic greenfinches or squirrels! Red baskets seem to attract more birds, by the way.

You can also put out fat, especially suet; coconut (but not desiccated coconut, nor dry bread, as both can harm birds) and apples which are great for attracting thrushes. Don't forget to put some food on the ground too, for the species that don't visit the table, but keep it well away from bushes where cats can lurk, and don't put fat too near windows or on paths!

Water is just as important, and you may be surprised to see birds bathing even with snow on the ground. You should provide water in a suitable container all year round, but food only between October and early spring when birds start to nest: some foods can be very harmful to young birds. Birds may become very dependent on you, so don't suddenly stop putting out food or water.

Nest boxes

are another good way of helping birds: this time by providing nest sites. Many birds, including blue tits, robins and even owls, will use boxes of suitable designs: write to the RSPB to find out how to make them, or where to buy them.

Ponds

are attractive to look at, and can hold a great mixture of wildlife. If you want to make one, butyl rubber makes the best liner or base for the pond, and comes complete with instructions, but it is a good idea to research the subject from books before you start such a large project. You need lots of time and effort to dig the pond, and thoroughly line it with layers of fine sand, old carpets or newspapers before putting down the liner, which should then be protected from above with more sand. Don't use sand from a beach or estuary as

it is too salty, and don't forget to remove any tacks or staples from the carpets!

When filled with water, the sand inside the pond will make it look like a revolting soup for a week or two, but it will eventually settle. Gardening books will tell you the best plants to stock it with and your local conservation group will have ideas on collecting frogspawn and encouraging frogs. You may need to keep a net over your pond, or site it where cats, dogs, and your little brother or sister cannot reach it.

Plants

the right plants encourage wildlife. Thick hedges make great homes for birds, insects and small mammals. Berry-bearing bushes, e.g. hawthorn, holly, cotoneaster and berberis (to name only a few) all attract birds in autumn and winter, as will the seeds left by sunflowers and michaelmas daisies. A buddleia bush is excellent for attracting insects, especially butterflies, as are many other flowers you can plant. Chris Baines' and Tony Soper's books both contain lots of good ideas.

Join a conservation task force

or set up one with your Guide Company. There's lots of useful conservation work to be done outside the garden. Why not tackle a piece of disused land near you? This may be complicated: whose land is it, and do they want it 'improved'? So call in the British Trust for Conservation Volunteers (formerly called the Conservation Corps) or someone else who knows what they're doing, such as a local nature reserve warden, to advise you.

You should then draw up a plan of action and a timetable, and make sure that you have the resources both for the present and to continue looking after the land in the future. You could start with a simple project like clearing an area of litter or rubbish. More complex tasks might include making a pond or hedge, clearing a canal, or managing a piece of grassland or woodland. In many places old vegetation may need to be cleared, and a diversity of plants introduced. If you are planting trees, you must take into account the type of soil and situation of your site; how large the trees will grow, what species are suitable (and available) and find out when to plant them. Expert advice really is essential: even a grassy wildflower meadow needs careful planning and management. You may find such practical conservation hard work, but very invigorating and rewarding.

Perhaps some of this advice seems a bit vague, but remember that if enough people follow these examples, there is a real chance of making change on a global scale. If enough people boycott the use of aerosols, for example, manufacturers would be forced to produce alternatives. If everyone joined the World Wildlife Fund, think how many nature reserves we could buy!

Why not join one of the many conservation societies that exist, and add your voice to theirs? Join your local naturalist trust, and see what other groups like the National Trust, the RSPB, the World Wildlife Fund and WATCH have to offer. Here are some useful addresses and books: your library will help you find more.

How to Make a Wildlife Garden by Chris Baines (Elm Tree)
The Bird Table Book by Tony Soper (good on wildlife gardening in general) (David & Charles).
Projects in Conservation D I Williams & D Anglesea (Wayland).
British Trust for Conservation Volunteers Project Pack, an excellent set of project cards, full of illustrations and practical advice.

British Trust for
Conservation Volunteers
36 St Mary's Street
Wallingford
Oxfordshire
OX10 0EU

The World Wildlife
Fund UK
Panda House
11–13 Ockford Road
Godalming
Surrey
GU7 1QU

Royal Society for the
Protection of Birds
The Lodge
Sandy
Bedfordshire
SG19 2DL

Royal Society for
Nature Conservation
22 The Green
Nettleham
Lincoln
LN2 2NR
For addresses of local
trusts, and WATCH

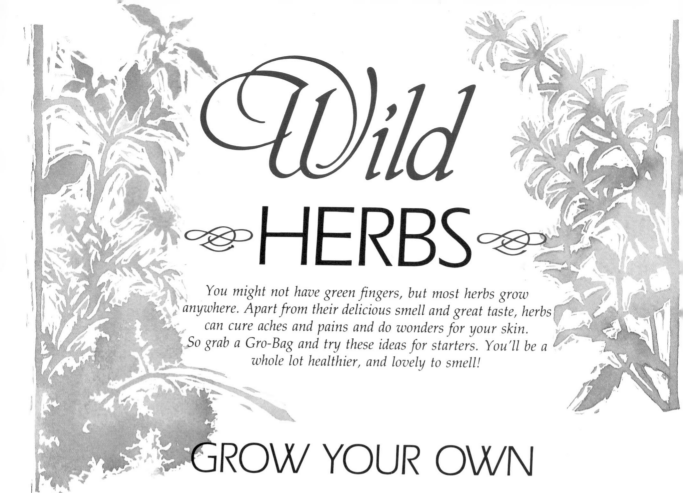

Wild HERBS

You might not have green fingers, but most herbs grow anywhere. Apart from their delicious smell and great taste, herbs can cure aches and pains and do wonders for your skin. So grab a Gro-Bag and try these ideas for starters. You'll be a whole lot healthier, and lovely to smell!

GROW YOUR OWN

by Gill Pawley
illustrations Julia Rowntree

There really is something special about growing your own herbs. If you're into cooking, a herb garden may be a necessity – some cooks find it unthinkable to use dried herbs and plenty of gardeners wouldn't dream of leaving herbs out of their gardens. Some plants flower at certain times of the year and most give off a lovely aroma, ranging from the pungent and heady, to the delicate and flowery. A herb garden can also produce a stunning splash of colour, with blue chicory, purple chive flowers, white woodsorrel and golden dandelions. Even without a large garden you can grow herbs in plant pots, troughs or Gro-Bags. If your kitchen has a sunny window ledge, you'll probably have the ideal spot for a few pots of herbs. You'll also get a deliciously aromatic kitchen for free.

Herbs are now more widely available than ever. Garden centres, larger supermarkets and greengrocers often stock the more common ones which are cheap and easy to grow. But which herbs are best? You could stick to the well-known varieties below, which are most useful in cooking and generally don't need much looking after, or why not try lovage, tarragon, oregano, dill or sorrel?

Basil is a particular favourite of cooks who enjoy Italian food – the one without the other is unthinkable! The basil plant has a warm, pungent aroma and delicate white flowers which should be removed regularly so that the plant produces healthy leaves throughout the year until autumn.

Sage There are many varieties, and it will grow anywhere! Sage is strong tasting and should be used sparingly; the furry leaves give off an equally strong aroma when rubbed.

Rosemary has been with us for centuries – Ophelia in *Hamlet* talks of rosemary 'for remembrance'. The leaves of the plant are thin and spiky, so it's a good idea to chop them to stop them getting stuck between your teeth! The plant will grow into a small sturdy bush and provide fresh rosemary all year.

Garden thyme has a strong, warm flavour and can be dried easily, so it is a good one to bear in mind if you have limited space and want to get the most from your plants.

Parsley is an old favourite. It is very easy to grow and can be used in many dishes. It likes deep soil and is a biennial, which means it will only live for two seasons. It's a good idea therefore to grow parsley from seed, sowing twice a year to give you fresh leaves as long as possible.

Pot marjoram is probably the most suitable of the three varieties of marjoram available. It will spread over any space it can, so you may need to keep it in check!

Some herbs are particularly good for drying, but the process calls for care and can be complex. Why not get a specialist book from the library or speak to someone who has tackled the job themselves? A bunch of herbs hung from the ceiling or a hook on the wall will perfume a room as well as looking decorative while it's drying.

COOKING WITH HERBS

The addition of herbs can make a basic meal something special. Some dishes and herbs are just made for each other. For special recipes see the book list, but meanwhile, try enhancing your cooking with some of these tips:

- Rosemary sprinkled on a leg of lamb before cooking complements the flavour of the meat.
- Hedge garlic adds a delicious tang to salads or dressings.
- A couple of bay leaves are a welcome addition to a casserole.
- Basil and Italian food are great friends; in fact it goes particularly well with anything tomatoey.
- Add a couple of sprigs of mint to the water of new potatoes before cooking.
- For a subtle salad dressing, add a couple of sprigs of tarragon to a bottle of wine vinegar. Or make a salad using chicory, fennel and nasturtium leaves. You can even use chopped young dandelion leaves.

BEAUTY WITH HERBS

The healing properties of herbs are well documented. You've probably used some yourself. If you're stung by a nettle there's always a dock leaf nearby which works as an antidote. Chamomile will grow anywhere and is well-known for its soothing properties. It can be used in compresses for wounds and burns, in the same way that we use anti-inflammatory creams. Raspberry leaves make a good mouthwash and the fruit juice is said to make you sleep well. With the introduction of drugs, the use of herbal remedies declined rapidly. But recently there's been a resurgence in the number of people using herbal treatments – just look at all the health food shops in your area.

Herbs have always been popular in beauty treatments. The basis of many preparations is an essential oil, which often comes from herbs. The essential oil is a liquid part of the plant cell and usually has a pleasant fragrance – hence its popular use in cosmetics. Aromatherapy's also big news now – the use of essential oils as direct treatment for aches and pains. It's especially effective to use an essential oil in massage. In this way, both the fragrance and the healing properties of the herb are used to their best advantage. To find out more, see the book list. The Body Shop sells a whole range of massage oils with different aromas for different moods.

Some beauty treatments are much simpler and can be tried out at home. Facial saunas are a good way of getting rid of impurities and dirt from the skin. Everyday grime can become embedded in the pores and sometimes no amount of cleansing can remove it – you need a treatment that opens up the pores. (Don't try this if you have very delicate or sensitive skin.)

Place some fresh herbs in a bowl and cover with boiling water. Put a towel over your head and lean over the bowl. Steam your face gently for ten minutes to leave your skin feeling fresh and glowing. Then splash your face with cold water and moisturise. What herbs to use depends on your skin type: for normal skin use lavender, elderflower or peppermint; for oily skin use mint, chamomile or rosemary and those with dry skin should try sage, comfrey or fennel.

Many bubble baths and bath oils are strong detergents which instead of soothing the skin, can actually dry it out. If you want a gentler addition to your bath water, fill a small bag of muslin with a selection of herbs, such as thyme, rosemary and chamomile. Immerse the bag as you run the bath water. If you want a particularly soothing bath, add a handful of chamomile leaves.

Herbs can be used to treat all kinds of ailments. For example, chamomile can help digestive disorders, rosemary is used in ointments to relieve pain from rheumatism and sage can be used in the treatment of liver diseases. Naturally, herbs should only be used in this way by someone who is qualified and knows what he or she is doing. If this interests you, try the book list below or your library.

For more details of the medicinal properties of herbs, try to get hold of *Herbs* by Dr Frantisek Stary and Dr Vaclav Jirasek (Hamlyn). There are many books on cooking with herbs, but Delia Smith's *Cookery Course* (BBC) is particularly good.

For more information about aromatherapy, see *The Body Shop Book* (Futura). The Body Shop also sells many cosmetics and beauty preparations using the potential of herbs to the full. Your local branch will advise you on what's best suited to your skin type.

Finally, *Kitty Little's Book of Herbal Beauty* (Penguin) gives lots of recipes for home treatments using herbs.

NAUTICAL KNIT

Deck yourself out landlubbers in our knit-it-yourself jumper and head for the nearest seaside.
This idiot-proof pattern is easy to follow and you should see quick results, as it's knitted on large needles with chunky wool.
You don't have to stick to our colour scheme either (although we think it's dead cool!). Why not try navy with a white stripe and red buttons?
The pattern is calculated for a medium/large. If you want a size smaller, follow the figures in brackets.
For the complete look, don deck shoes, stripy leggings and a sailor hat. Anchors away!

by Clarissa Dann
photographs David Woolford
make-up Lisa Miller
styling Susannah Marriott

Materials
1 pair size 4½mm, 1 pair size 5½mm needles.
9 (8) 50g balls cream and 5 (4) 50g balls navy *chunky* yarn. We used Phildar Shoot 248, a machine washable 75% acrylic 25% wool mix. Jaeger Superwash Sport pure wool is also suitable and machine washable although more expensive.
3 × 3½mm cream buttons with large loops to get a wool darning needle through.
1 large-eyed wool darning needle for sewing up the pieces.

Measurements

	Medium/Large	Small
Length from neck to base	69cm	64cm
Bust width	109cm	102cm
Length of sleeve seam	56cm	51cm

Tension
Using size 5½mm needles, cast on 30 stitches and work 40 rows. Count out 19 stitches and measure the width across the row. Then count out 26 rows and measure the length of these rows. Both measurements should be 12cm. If the measurements are greater or smaller than this, change to smaller or larger needles (yes that way round!) and try again until you are sure you have the right tension.

Abbreviations
k=knit; p=purl; st(s)=stitch(es); inc=increase (knit or purl into front and back of next stitch); dec=decrease (knit or purl next two stitches together); tog=together; beg=beginning; patt=pattern (8 rows cream and 2 rows navy in stocking stitch); sl=slip 1 stitch; psso=pass slipped stitch over; n=navy; c=cream; cont=continue; rep=repeat; sto st=stocking stitch (knit 1 row purl 1 row); rem=remaining.

General hints
Do not carry the navy yarn up the 8 rows of cream for each stripe. Break it after each navy stripe is complete, making sure that you don't lose the last stitch by leaving too short an end. Count how many stitches you have got on the needle at regular intervals (particularly when increasing on the sleeves): it does save more time in the long run!

Back
Using size 4½mm needles and n, cast on 80 (74) sts. Work 19 rows in k1 p1 ribbing.
Next row: rib 11 (10) inc, rib 11 (10) inc, rib 12 (11) inc, rib 12 (12) inc, rib 12 (11) inc, rib 11 (10) inc, rib 11 (10). You should have 86 (80) sts.
Change to size 5½mm needles and work 8 rows c, 2 rows n sto st until 13th (12th) stripe has been completed.
Shape neck and shoulders
Row 1: Cast off 4 sts, patt 32 (30), cast off 14 (12), patt 36 (34). On 36 (34) sts:
Row 2: Cast off 4 sts, patt to end.
Row 3: Cast off 3 sts, patt to end.
Rows 4–5: As rows 2–3.

Row 6: Cast off 4 sts, patt to end.
Row 7: Cast off 2 sts, patt to end.
Cast off rem sts.
Rejoin yarn to rem sts at neck edge and work rows 3 to end.

Front
Using size 4½mm needles, cast on 74 (68) sts. Work 19 rows in k1 p1 rib.
Next row: rib 12 (11) inc, rib 12 (11) inc, rib 13 (12) inc, rib 13 (12) inc, rib 12 (11) inc, rib 12 (11). You should have 79 (73) sts.
Change to size 5½mm needles, and work 8 rows c, 2 rows n, then 8 rows c again in sto st. Change to n.
Row 19: Cast on 6 sts and k 85 (69).
Row 20: p 79 (73) inc 1, p 6 to form 86 (80) sts.
Cont working 8 rows c, 2 rows n sto st until 12th (11th) n stripe has been completed (counting right from beg of sto st work). Change to c.
Shape neck and shoulders
Row 1: patt 36 (34), cast off 14 (12) sts, patt 36. On 36 sts:
Row 2: patt to end.
Row 3: dec 1 at neck edge, patt to end.
Rows 4–7: As rows 2–3.
Row 8: patt to end.
Row 9: Change to n, dec 1 at neck edge.
Row 10: p to end.
Row 11: Change to c, dec 1 at neck edge, patt to end.
Row 12: Cast off 4, patt to end.
Rows 13–16: As 11–12.
Row 17: dec 1, patt to end.
Cast off rem sts.
Rejoin yarn to rem sts at neck edge and work rows 3 to end.

Front flap
Pick up 30 sts vertically from squared-out edge (see diagram above), sl 1 from horizontal edge above, psso, sl next st from horizontal edge above. You should have 31 sts now. Using n:
Row 1: k2 tog, p1 k1 rib to end.
Row 2: Rib 30, sl 1 from edge above, psso, sl 1 from edge above.
Row 3: k2 tog, rib to end.